Published in Pasadena, CA by Bethke Writings. Bethke Writings titles may be purchased in bulk for educational, business, fund-raising, or sales promotional use. For information, please e-mail info@bethkewritings.com.

Special thanks to Wheelhouse Creative for the book design, and Jeremy Maxfield as editor.

Scripture quotations are from the ESV® Bible (The Holy Bible, English Standard Version®), copyright © 2001 by Crossway, a publishing ministry of Good News Publishers. Used by permission. All rights reserved."

Scripture quotations marked CSB®, are taken from the Christian Standard Bible®, Copyright © 2017 by Holman Bible Publishers. Used by permission. Christian Standard Bible®, and CSB® are federally registered trademarks of Holman Bible Publishers.

The Library of Congress Cataloging-in-Publication Data is on file with the Library of Congress
ISBN-13: 978-0692858301

How to get the most out of this book

First, thank you. Thanks for reading and being willing to take this journey with your spouse or significant other. We hope these books serve as a catalyst of change, or simply an encouragement to your already strong marriage.

To get the most out of this book, we suggest a few things. First, we want to acknowledge that every marriage is different. There are different needs, nuances, callings, and circumstances. And finding God's good way and rhythm in *your unique marriage* is the fastest way to true joy. And so that means there might be a few suggestions or notes or thoughts in these books that actually don't work very well for your and your husband.

And that's ok. We want you to know you have to permission to adapt and change and use this book in whatever way best serves you two. If there's a suggestion we give that worked great for us, but it didn't for you, forget it. We want these books to serve you primarily, and not shame you or make you think you aren't 'doing something right' if something we say doesn't work for you guys.

Also, as you read you'll notice we set these books up to work best on a weekly basis (i.e. one topic per week). But feel free to change that, slow it down, speed it up, etc.

Lastly, the workbook sections mention when the section is meant to be done individually, and also collectively, so keep an eye out for that.

We hope you enjoy taking this journey with us and we'd love for you to say hi on social media if you're enjoying it or it's an encouragement!

Jeff & Alyssa

PS: Don't forget to watch the corresponding Love That Lasts videos with our twelve sets of mentors while you read along as well. The books are great by themselves, but we envisioned them working best alongside the video series. If you don't know what that is, Jeff and I had the chance to interview twelve sets of married mentors who are experts on a particular topic (some you might know like Korie and Willie Robertson from Duck Dynasty or Drs. Les and Leslie Parrott). If you don't have the videos and you'd like to get them, visit lovethatlasts.co/video. You will also receive a code to take the Deep Love assessment, which is a custom ten-page report on your relationship. Also use code "videoseries" at lovethatlasts.co/video and it will take 25% off for you as a thank you.

JEFF

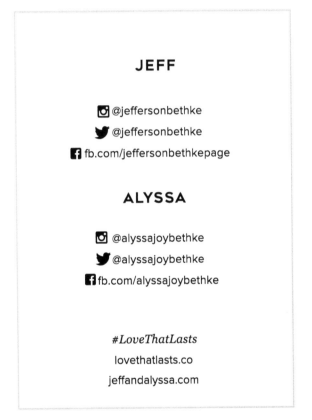

📷 @jeffersonbethke

🐦 @jeffersonbethke

f fb.com/jeffersonbethkepage

ALYSSA

📷 @alyssajoybethke

🐦 @alyssajoybethke

f fb.com/alyssajoybethke

#LoveThatLasts

lovethatlasts.co

jeffandalyssa.com

Theology
of
Marriage

01

"Mawwiage. Mawwiage is what bwings us togethew today. Mawwiage, that bwessed awwangement, that dweam within a dweam. And wove, twue wove, wiww fowwow you fowevah and evah...so tweasuwe youw wove." —Princess Bride

I was in my white dress. My bodice was covered with silver rhinestones and my skirt flowed out in white tulle. Before me stood my soon-to-be husband, strong, handsome, and tall. He held my hands, and we exchanged vows as the rain poured behind us. Our family and friends witnessed it, and tears spilled over both of our cheeks as we committed to love, serve, and cherish one another for the rest of our days. It was a holy moment, and one that I will forever cherish.

I knew God was smiling at us that day, reveling in our commitment and rejoicing at what He had done. How He had taken two people made in His image who had turned their backs on Him, but who surrendered their lives to their Creator later on in life. Two souls who now were secure in Jesus, two souls who would need Jesus every day after, and who would desperately need Him to keep the vows that flowed from their lips. He knew what our journey would look like, but He also knew that we needed each other to continue this journey.

Ever since I was a little girl, I longed to be married. My parents have a great, strong marriage and I wanted what they had. I wanted to be a mom one day, to have a household to care for, to laugh with my husband the way my mom did with my dad, and someone to do life with. I mean, when I was five, I was a bride for Halloween! Most women I know want to get married because, I believe, God created us that way. We weren't made to live alone, and whether it be family or best friends, or marriage, we are meant to live in community. We are created out of community (the Trinity) for community. God created male and female, and purposed for them to be married, and to go out on mission with each other.

Genesis 1:26-28 (NIV) says, *"Then God said, "Let us make mankind in our image, in our likeness, so that they may rule over the fish in the sea and the birds in the sky, over the livestock and all the wild animals, and over all the creatures that move along the ground."*

So God created mankind in his own image,
in the image of God he created them;
male and female he created them.

God blessed them and said to them, "Be fruitful and increase in number; fill the earth and subdue it. Rule over the fish in the sea and the birds in the sky and over every living creature that moves on the ground."

Notice how God created both male and female in His image. Both are needed to complete the full image of God, so when we come together in marriage, we are fully representing Him. We are made with the same intentionality, same worth and value, but with different roles, natures, strengths, and weaknesses. We need each other to show the world Christ. (Please note that you don't have to be married to be complete. Sometimes God calls people to be single, or for some reason some remain single even though they'd love to be married. God is writing a good story for you and is using you in mighty ways. You can go and do things that you can't do when you're married, and you are complete in Jesus. We all are. Our husbands do not complete us.)

Marriage was God's idea and it is good. It shows the world who God is, and helps us to understand His nature. It draws us out of ourselves, challenges us, sanctifies us, and provides sweet fellowship. Within marriage, we are fully known and fully loved. As the author C.S. Lewis writes in *The Four Loves:*

"To love at all is to be vulnerable. Love anything and your heart will be wrung and possibly broken. If you want to make sure of keeping it intact you must give it to no one, not even an animal. Wrap it carefully round with hobbies and little luxuries; avoid all entanglements. Lock it up safe in the casket or coffin of your selfishness. But in that casket, safe, dark, motionless, airless, it will change. It will not be broken; it will become unbreakable, impenetrable, irredeemable. To love is to be vulnerable."

The marriage covenant allows us to fully put down our barriers and defenses, and be our true selves. We can stop the striving, doubting, worrying. We don't have to fear our spouse truly knowing us and walking away because they have promised to be with us until death. And vice versa. That's the difference between living together and marriage. When you live together, you're doing all the things married people do, which sounds so exciting, but it's without any commitment. Deep down, in the middle of the night when you're alone with your thoughts, you have no assurance that they'll stay. You can't fully let your guard down because there's no promise holding your relationship together. Either one of you could just change your mind on any day and that's that. You're playing marriage, but without any of the peace and true joy that comes along with it.

I remember the first fight Jeff and I had when we were married. I can't remember what it was about, but it was the first time that Jeff saw the real me. Not that I hid things from him when we dated at all, but this time he saw how messy I can be. When we dated, if something hurt me or I was confused about a conversation, I could go home and cry myself to sleep. Now that we were married, there was no escaping off by myself. I couldn't cry to sleep anymore without him knowing. He was there and he could tell whenever something was off or wrong with me. Anyway, we had a fight, and I said hurtful things that I didn't mean and walked off, and he was really upset with me. I remember after a few minutes of both of us cooling down for a bit, he came to find me and I had this thought, "I bet he doesn't even want to be married to me anymore. I did it this time. He finally saw my true colors." As I confessed this to him, he laughed and looked me right in the eye, "Lyss, I'm not going anywhere. I'm right here forever. I love you and I'm committed to loving you for the rest of my life." It was in that moment that I knew he meant every word. He wasn't going anywhere. No matter what. And neither was I. We had made a promise and we were sticking to it.

In his book, *The Meaning of Marriage,* Timothy Keller writes about the mission of marriage:

"Within this Christian vision for marriage, here's what it means to fall in love. It is to look at another person and get a glimpse of the person God is creating and to say, 'I see who God is making you, and it excites me! I want to be part of that. I want to partner with you and God in the journey you are taking to his throne. And when we get there, I will look at your magnificence and say, 'I always knew you could be like this. I got glimpses of it on earth, but now look at you!' Each spouse should see the great thing that Jesus is doing in the life of their mate through the Word, the gospel. Each spouse then should give him-or herself to be a vehicle for that work and envision the day that you will stand together before God, seeing each other presented in spotless beauty and glory."

What a beautiful picture of marriage! Yes, this is what it's all about. You know that no matter the struggles and weaknesses that both of you have, underneath them all, God is growing you and using your spouse to make you more like Jesus. Don't lose the vision. Don't give up hope. You are making each other into your true selves.

In your marriage, you and your spouse are both called on a mission together. To make Jesus known. To be better together than apart. What is God calling the two to do? How can you make Him famous as a couple? There's a reason He's brought you and your husband together. You both possess qualities that are needed to not only make you both more like Jesus, but to embody Jesus to the world. God gave Adam and Eve to garden and cultivate, and so He has given you and your spouse a garden to work as well. It might not be an actual garden, but there is work that He has for the both of you to do together, as a team.

Marriage is two individuals coming together to make God known on this earth. To be committed to each other's holiness, to fight hard to cheer each other on, learn to communicate, work through conflict, do this life as you learn to become one. It involves a lot of sacrifice, long nights, hard talks, prayers, and dying to self. But it also involves a whole lot of laughs, adventures, crazy God moments, and becoming the person God created you to be as you learn to put someone above yourself, and be committed to them for the rest of you life.

GUIDEBOOK

Theology of Marriage

"HAVEN'T YOU READ," [JESUS] REPLIED, "THAT HE WHO CREATED THEM IN THE BEGINNING MADE THEM MALE AND FEMALE," AND HE ALSO SAID, "FOR THIS REASON A MAN WILL LEAVE HIS FATHER AND MOTHER AND BE JOINED TO HIS WIFE, AND THE TWO WILL BECOME ONE FLESH? SO THEY ARE NO LONGER TWO, BUT ONE FLESH. THEREFORE, WHAT GOD HAS JOINED TOGETHER, LET NO ONE SEPARATE."

Matthew 19:4-6 (CSB)

Those words are among the most familiar yet sacred realities echoed from one generation to the next. Chances are, you heard it right between "I do," and "you may now kiss the bride!" Most wedding ceremonies conclude with Jesus' words: "What God has joined together, let no one separate."

To highlight the unique nature of marriage, Jesus pointed all the way back to the first pages of Scripture and the first moments of human history. The Bible begins and ends with marriage: Adam and Eve in Genesis, Jesus and His church in Revelation.

In fact, if you could summarize the Bible succinctly, it would be about God creating, pursuing, and restoring a bride—a people for Himself, called into oneness with Him and with each other.

You read in the previous pages that you are created in the image of God and that marriage is a picture of God's love. It's the closest thing you can experience in this world to the joy and satisfaction of God's unconditional goodness.

So, before digging into the specific topics addressed in this workbook, some groundwork needs to be done in order to experience the joy of a flourishing marriage. Each week, we're going to start this section of the workbook with the words of Jesus. If we want to know joy, and flourishing, and beauty, it comes from him. He reveals the truth to us— the truth about who God is and about who we are—who we were created to be.

Write your favorite quote,
song lyric, or Bible
verse related to love or
marriage. If you're extra
artistic, get creative with
your handwriting or draw
something to represent love.

First of all, there is no fairytale relationship. Prince Charming doesn't exist. There's no riding into the sunset as the credits roll. Nobody is perfect and sometimes life is kind of boring, right? You'll have plenty of days filled with doing chores, paying bills, and wondering what that funny smell is. And that's the secret to a full life--finding joy in the mundane. Life doesn't fade into *happily ever after* once you say, "I do." The closest life gets to a rom-com is when you have the ability to laugh at and learn from your mistakes, finding the joy in the ordinary parts of your life.

This shouldn't be depressing. It's actually more romantic to recognize that out of everyone in the world, you chose your husband and he chose you! You weren't fated for *the one* (and you don't have to wonder if you found the one, which is one of the most dangerous ideas in our culture). You said, *You're the one I give my love to from this day on.* Choosing— and keeping that promise to continue choosing—to love someone for the rest of your life is crazy romantic. It's a commitment, not just for those beautiful moments of richer and better and in health, but in the mundane and even painful moments too. *Until death do you part.*

So if you are asking yourself the question that our culture is obsessed with, *Is he the one?* think about the simple counsel summed up in a tweet I saw recently:

> *How to know if you are married to the right person. Short answer: Look at the name on the marriage certificate.*

Love is commitment. You choose it every day. And nothing is as satisfying as a no-matter-what kind of love.

Think back to when you got married.

- **What is your favorite memory of the proposal?**

_____

_____

_____

_____

- **How did you know he was the one?**

_____

_____

_____

_____

- **What is your favorite memory of the wedding?**

_____

_____

_____

- **What is your favorite memory of your first days together as husband and wife?**

_____

_____

_____

- What are some of the normal, everyday lessons you had to learn about life together?

  _____

  _____

  _____

  _____

- Think back over your vows. You may have written your own or used something more traditional, but think about these ideas: _for better, for worse, for richer, for poorer, in sickness and health ..._

  _____

  _____

  _____

- What is something that you love about your husband even more now than you did before getting married?

  _____

  _____

  _____

- What is the hardest thing you've faced together?

  _____

  _____

  _____

• How did you grow from it?

_____

_____

_____

• What is the best thing you've experienced together?

_____

_____

_____

• If you wrote your own vows, think back to what you chose to say. Why did you want to be sure to say those things?

_____

_____

_____

_____

• What is something that you love about your husband even more now than you did before getting married?

_____

_____

_____

_____

First Corinthians 13 is often called the love chapter, so there's a good chance that someone read it aloud at your wedding. A friend of ours, Derwin Gray, who is in the *Theology of Marriage* video with his wife, Vicki, has a great way to encourage people to really meditate (or *marinate*, as he would say) on true, biblical, Christ-like, no-matter-what love. As a pastor, Derwin personalizes this chapter, asking people to use their names every time it says *love*. Try it out!

- **Write your name in the blanks below.**

_____ is patient, _____ is kind.
{ love }   { love }

_____ does not envy, is not boastful, is not arrogant,
{ love }

is not rude, is not self-seeking, is not irritable, and does not keep a record

of wrongs. _____ finds no joy in unrighteousness but
{ love }

rejoices in the truth. _____ bears all things, believes
{ love }

all things, hopes all things, endures all things.

1 Corinthians 13:4-7 (CSB)

Your marriage ultimately isn't about you. When people see you they will get a glimpse of the greatest love—Jesus. We know what love is because we know who Love is.

That sounds great, but if you're anything like me, then you know a lot of those things aren't always true about yourself. You're not always patient or kind. Sometimes you are selfish and irritable and jealous. But think about how amazing this is: Remember how we said at the beginning that as men and women created in the image of God, our love is a reflection of His love for us? Read back through those same verses but put the name *God* in each blank.

Are you starting to understand God's love for you? Are you starting to see how when your eyes are opened to this all-encompassing and perfect love, your view of marriage and of your spouse is radically transformed. It's like the light has just been turned on and you are seeing the infinite possibilities for loving and for being loved. When you open yourself up, allowing the love of God to fill your heart, it will spill over in the way you love others—especially your spouse. Your marriage will become a picture of God's love for all to see.

Remind yourself of those verses all week. Maybe you want to start each morning by reading these verses as a prayer. Make reminders around your home, in your car, or on your phone. These are great verses to memorize. (Any of the proverbs or words of Jesus you will read each week are great to memorize too.)

"WHEN OVER THE YEARS SOMEONE HAS SEEN YOU AT YOUR WORST, AND KNOWS YOU WITH ALL YOUR STRENGTHS AND FLAWS, YET COMMITS HIM- OR HERSELF TO YOU WHOLLY, IT IS A CONSUMMATE EXPERIENCE. TO BE LOVED BUT NOT KNOWN IS COMFORTING BUT SUPERFICIAL. TO BE KNOWN AND NOT LOVED IS OUR GREATEST FEAR. BUT TO BE FULLY KNOWN AND TRULY LOVED IS, WELL, A LOT LIKE BEING LOVED BY GOD. IT IS WHAT WE NEED MORE THAN ANYTHING. IT LIBERATES US FROM PRETENSE, HUMBLES US OUT OF OUR SELF-RIGHTEOUSNESS, AND FORTIFIES US FOR ANY DIFFICULTY LIFE CAN THROW AT US."

- Tim Keller,
from *Meaning of Marriage*

Make this time together each week special—it's a date night! Turn off your phones and give all of your attention to each other.

- Ask each other about the things you read and wrote about in the "on your own" section on the previous pages. Remember that this is a conversation with your husband. Enjoy it! This exercise each week isn't about interviewing your spouse or checking answers; it's about getting to know each other and developing a habit of meaningful time together.

- Go to *Love That Lasts* in your library at *bethkeworkshops.com* and watch this week's video: Theology of Marriage with Derwin and Vicki Gray. Then, ask each other what was most interesting, most challenging, and your big takeaway from the video. Use the video sidebar to take notes and to help your conversation.

- Plan another night this week to invite a couple over for dinner, ideally an older couple or friends who have been married longer than you have. Share with them that you may be asking them questions as you go through this series. Reading the book, watching the videos, completing the workbook, and talking to friends or mentors will help you see your relationship through different eyes.

Proverbs 15:22 says, "Without counsel plans fail, but with many advisers they succeed." Obviously, you want the best marriage possible, so invite others into this experience—and into your life beyond the time it takes you to go through this workbook.

Theology of Marriage with

Derwin & Vicki Gray

This section is a place to take notes if you also purchased the 12 corresponding video sessions from our 12 mentors. What did they say that resonated with you? What was your favorite part? What was most challenging?

_____

_____

_____

_____

_____

_____

_____

_____

_____

_____

_____

_____

_____

If you don't have this video
you can purchase it at

lovethatlasts.co/videoseries

Trust

02

Trust is foundational in any healthy relationship. This is not to say that you have a naïve trust in your boyfriend or husband, but that you are able to trust him completely. That he's a man of integrity and is trustworthy. Many unhealthy relationships happen when trust is not at the foundation because it's been broken, and often it's been broken time and time again. If this is true in a marriage, then there is still hope and healing when both partners are humble, repentant, and forgiving. When there's support and counseling and humility so the trust can be rebuilt. If, however, the trust is broken while dating or engaged, then it's probably best to get out. Take a break. Let them go. Because if you can't trust him while dating, you certainly won't be able to trust him while married.

Trust is so foundational to a healthy relationship because it takes risks and vulnerability and fully leaning into one another. If there's no trust, then it prevents from you being one, which is the whole point of marriage. To give yourself to another, to sacrifice and serve, to learn and grow and become more like Jesus through it all.

I remember the summer right before Jeff and I started dating (the second time), I was at my friend's wedding. All of us ladies were in the suite of this gorgeous hotel overlooking the water getting ready for her big day. My mom and I were talking to the bride and her mom, hearing more detail of how her love story with her soon-to-be-husband unfolded. My sweet friend had gone through a devastating break up with a boy before meeting her now husband. After her break up, she realized how important it was for her husband to be a man of humility and teachability. Her mom looked at my mom and said, "You know all of the other things that I had been praying for my daughter's future husband could be learned or grown like leading her well or pursuing her heart and being if he's teachable and humble. That really is the most important." That stayed with my heart ever since and I started to pray that for my future husband constantly.

When Jeff got down on one knee and asked me to be his wife 9 months later, I knew without hesitation that he was a man of humility and was so teachable. He had proven it over and over, and continues to, to this day. It's what I love most about him. Whenever Jeff and I get into an argument, he is always the first to come to me and ask for forgiveness, regardless of who was primarily in the wrong. He seeks mentors out, is open with them and asks them for their wisdom and direction in whatever he is facing. These two qualities make it easy for me to trust Jeff in the big picture aspect of our marriage, as well as in all the little details. I trust that he will do whatever he says he will do, and I can trust that when he's passionate about something that he wants our family to implement, he has thought long and hard and sought counsel on the matter.

One of the most poignant ways these qualities play out in our marriage is when it comes to trusting his faithfulness to me. When I was 7 months pregnant with our first baby, Jeff took me to Victoria B.C. for our babymoon. I had always dreamed of staying at the Empress Hotel and having high tea there. Bucket-list item for sure. So Jeff surprised me with a three-night stay there, and we had high tea every afternoon! I loved that trip, not so much because it was a dream come true or because of how amazing I felt when my belly floated in that indoor pool (and all the pregnant ladies said amen) but because it was the sweetest three days to talk about all our hopes and excitements and fears of being new parents. Jeff confessed some of his fears, which I never would have guessed.

One morning we were sitting on the couch in our room overlooking the cloudy city with tea in our hands, and Jeff turned to me and said, "Hey Lyss. I need to tell you something." And he went on to confess how he hadn't been pure with his eyes the night before on social media, and his thoughts hadn't been pure and holy. He admitted that thoughts of the past were hitting him hard and asked not only for forgiveness but that I would pray over him and ask the Lord to do battle on his behalf. There's been a handful of times that has happened in our marriage and every time I love him more because of it, and my trust grows deeper. I don't get upset when he tells me or heap shame on him. But rather, I'm so thankful that the heart of my husband trusts me and is vulnerable and open. I don't have to doubt him, or guess if he's struggling in this area (which most guys do struggle in various ways). I know that when he's struggling, he'll come to me right away, and that I have full access to ask him the hard questions at any time. This honesty breathes life into any marriage because this is where true intimacy happens. When both people can be completely honest in front of one another, and know that the other will welcome them in as they are. We are a team, growing and fighting for holiness together.

So here's the mantra that Jeff and I live by in our marriage: Deal in the light. Don't hold anything in the dark. Don't hide things from each other. Don't let things go under the rug to only build up bitterness. Don't lie. Don't withhold truth. Be forthcoming, and do so as soon as possible. When you sin, confess it right away. Don't believe that lie that Satan throws at you—that you should remain isolated and alone. When you're struggling with something, go to your husband and tell him. Ask him to pray for you. God gave you to each other to be a team, and truly two are better than one.

The reality is that no matter how healthy your relationship is, your man will fail you and sin against you, whether it be in little ways or a big way. Each day we wake up with the decision to follow God and choose our spouse. And each day that decision is played out in a million ways. Some days he won't choose to follow Jesus or choose you. And same goes with you. Because we're selfish, and human and in need of a Savior. In Christ though, we have hope. So deal in the light, but also run to Jesus. Pour out your heart to Him, pray for your husband or boyfriend, entrusting him to the Lord. The Holy Spirit is the one who changes and heals and convicts and grows two people close together. Continue to seek Him. You can trust your spouse when you're a believer because ultimately you know God is in control and He is the one who loves you more than anyone ever could, gives you your purpose and identity and life.

"For at one time you were darkness, but now you are light in the Lord. Walk as children of light (for the fruit of the light is found in all that is good and righteous and true), and try to discern what is pleasing to the Lord. Take no part in the unfruitful works of darkness, but instead expose them" (Ephesians 5:8-11).

Write your favorite quote, song lyric, or Bible verse related to trust. If you're extra artistic, get creative with your handwriting or draw something to represent trust.

GUIDEBOOK

Trust

02

"WHOEVER CAN BE TRUSTED WITH VERY LITTLE CAN ALSO BE TRUSTED WITH MUCH, AND WHOEVER IS DISHONEST WITH VERY LITTLE WILL ALSO BE DISHONEST WITH MUCH."

Luke 16:10 (NIV)

Trust is the key ingredient for any healthy relationship. You have to know that you can trust someone if you're ever going to move beyond a surface-level acquaintance. You may be the kind of person who opens up quickly; however, most people are slow to open up. Whether you dive in headfirst or you gradually test the waters, inching in a little bit deeper over a longer period of time, our hearts have been shaped by God for meaningful relationships.

Jesus told a parable about different servants who had been trusted with different investments from their master. He actually told a few variations of this story that you can read in Luke 16, 19 and Matthew 25. The point to the parables of talents and managers is about making wise decisions based on what you've been given. Ultimately, Jesus is referring to the gospel and our relationship with God. Are we taking what we know about God and valuing his blessings enough to do whatever we can to grow in relationship with Him? To make this point Jesus uses what we all know to be true—some people can be trusted with more than others and if you can't trust someone with simple things, you're crazy if you trust them with something of real value.

ON YOUR OWN

The principle of trustworthiness applies to every relationship, not just to your relationship with God and with your husband. Actually, they're going to all bleed into one another like a watercolor. There are no solid lines. There's no compartmentalizing trust into different areas. That's exactly what Jesus is saying about being faithful and trustworthy with a little and a lot. If you can't be trusted with friends or coworkers, how can you be trusted in a marriage? Below is an easy, but hopefully helpful, trustworthiness quiz. There is no 'failing' this test, but it is helpful to truly self assess how much trust you are building with your spouse.

USING A SCALE OF 1-10
(1 = NEVER, 10 = ALWAYS)

Answer the following questions.

How often do you remember to do what you say you'll do?

1 · 2 · 3 · 4 · 5 · 6 · 7 · 8 · 9 · 10

How often do you work hard?

1 · 2 · 3 · 4 · 5 · 6 · 7 · 8 · 9 · 10

How often do you make comments or talk about other people?

1 · 2 · 3 · 4 · 5 · 6 · 7 · 8 · 9 · 10

How often do you laugh at or make jokes about other people?

1 · 2 · 3 · 4 · 5 · 6 · 7 · 8 · 9 · 10

How often do people tell you secrets or personal things?

1 · 2 · 3 · 4 · 5 · 6 · 7 · 8 · 9 · 10

How often do people ask for your advice?

1 · 2 · 3 · 4 · 5 · 6 · 7 · 8 · 9 · 10

If you struggle with the small things like remembering things, making comments and jokes about people, working hard, you may want to dismiss them as not being a big deal, but they actually play into how other people see you and possibly even how they see the value of Jesus. The love of Jesus should transform our relationships.

What do you need to work on in order to be trustworthy in the "small" things?

_____

_____

_____

_____

Now think about the big things like being dishonest, hurtful, selfish, or unfaithful, and whether or not you are more or less trustworthy than you were in the past. Ask yourself what your attitudes and actions reveal about how much you value the gift of real relationships.

Think about a time that you were really hurt in a relationship. Think about a time when you've hurt somebody else. How have those experiences had a ripple effect in other relationships? Have you grown from those painful betrayals or have the caused you to be guarded?

_____

_____

_____

_____

_____

When you keep other people at a distance, it's the result of sin—either sin around you, within you, or both. Sin makes you hide. That's what you saw in the Garden of Eden (see Genesis 3). Adam and Eve sin, betray God's trust, try to hide, then make excuses and pass the blame to avoid the truth. By the way, how crazy is it to hide behind a tree from the Creator of heaven and earth? He knows *everything!*

That's actually exactly why God's infinite love for us is greater than anything we can fully wrap our finite minds around. He knows us *completely.* And yet even while knowing everything he loves us *completely.*

To really experience love means we have to know and be known. It requires honesty. We can't love someone we don't know. We can't be loved if we're putting up a fake image of who we really are. And it's out of being loved by God that we're able to love others.

As man and woman, husband and wife, created in the image of God, the person on this planet that you should trust the most is your husband. He should be able to trust you more than anyone else. Marriage should be a safe place where you can be transparent and vulnerable—naked and unashamed, literally and figuratively.

It's good to have other close friends, people who know you, people you trust, but no other friendship should be more honest and transparent than your marriage. Nobody should know you or your husband better than you know each other. Don't believe the lie that there are some things you just can't tell him.

Trust is key to any *healthy* relationship. If you want your marriage to flourish, you have to be trustworthy and to trust in the little and the big things. You've committed your life to him. He's committed his life to you. That's as big as it gets!

BEFORE YOUR DATE NIGHT DISCUSSION, DO TWO THINGS:

1. Get one of her favorite candies. You will surprise each other with a blind taste test; so keep it covered in a box or bag until you meet!

2. Think about some specific examples of ways that she has shown her trustworthiness—little and big things. Write them here.

_____

_____

_____

_____

_____

_____

_____

_____

_____

_____

_____

Intimacy is based on trust. True intimacy involves an exchange. Someone gives vulnerability, and the other person gives assurance and honor of that vulnerability back. Then reciprocation of that vulnerability happens, creating a beautiful cycle. And that bond is exclusive and hidden, only for the two to behold and be a part of.

Remember to turn off your phones and to give all of your attention to each other. Paying attention instead of being distracted by a phone, TV, etc. is a simple way to be trustworthy in a little thing. You are showing that you value one another.

- Sit together on the couch or at the table. Take turn closing your eyes while the other person gives you a taste of the candy they chose for you. No peeking and no wedding-cake-smashed-in-the-face shenanigans. This is about trust! Try to guess what kind of candy you tasted.
- Ask each other the following questions.

  - Were you nervous about blindly trusting me? Why? What made you believe or doubt that you could trust me in something fun like this?
  - In general, is trusting easy for you? Why?
  - Why do you trust me?
  - What are some of the little things that I do or that I can do that show you that I love you completely?
  - Is any topic of conversation or openness about something in your life strictly off limits when talking to a trusted friend or mentor? (It's important for you both to know what the expectation is here so that you never have a misunderstanding of breaking trust with one another.)
  - Do we need to stop criticizing, gossiping about, or making fun of other people? Do we ever try to justify gossip as concern, prayer requests, or normal conversation?
  - How does having a loving and trusting marriage encourage you to grow in your relationship with God? How can setting an example of trustworthiness in speech and action show others the love of Christ?

- Ask each other about any of the other things you read and wrote about in the "on your own" section on the previous pages. Remember, this is a conversation with your husband. Enjoy it!

- Go to *Love That Lasts* in your library at *bethkeworkshops.com* and watch this week's video: Trust with Melanie and Seth Studley. They have a pretty incredible story of almost divorcing, even though one of them was a marriage and family licensed counselor. They also host a marriage podcast called Stronger Marriages. After watching, ask each other what was most interesting, most challenging, and a big "takeaway" from the video. Use the video sidebar to take notes and to help your conversation.

- Pray together, thanking God for blessing you with a relationship with him and with one another. Ask for God's help in being thoughtful and trustworthy in everything you do out of gratitude for the gift of love.

A gossip betrays a confidence, but a
trustworthy person keeps a secret.
Proverbs 11:13 (NIV)

Trust with

Melanie & Seth Studley

This section is a place to take notes if you also purchased the
12 corresponding video sessions from our 12 mentors. What did
they say that resonated with you? What was your favorite part?
What was most challenging?

_____

_____

_____

_____

_____

_____

_____

_____

_____

_____

_____

_____

_____

_____

If you don't have this video
you can purchase it at

lovethatlasts.co/videoseries

Communication

03

Instead of useless classes like speech or algebra, I wish high schools required everyone to take a class on how to communicate in everyday life. With your friends, boss, coworkers, and future spouse. I personally would have loved to know how to enter into healthy conflict and not be a pushover at work. Communication is so important to learn how to do well in life, and it's so vital for your relationships. God wasn't joking when he said that there is life and death in the tongue (Proverbs 18:21). He also said in James 3:2, "For we all stumble in many ways. And if anyone does not stumble in what he says, he is a perfect man, able also to bridle his whole body."

Communication is hard enough, let alone with the opposite sex! Sometimes Jeff and I just misunderstand each other because we heard incorrectly or because we're both thinking different things, and other times we didn't communicate well enough. We didn't add a piece of information that would have been really helpful, or explain where we were coming from, or simply let each other in on something. I feel like most of our arguments are because one of us didn't communicate well enough.

Just last night, we got into a misunderstanding. Jeff was doing the dinner dishes while I was finishing up the laundry, vacuuming, and trying to get the kids ready for bed. Kins had a dirty diaper and I had been telling her I'd change it, but kept getting distracted by other things. Finally, as I was running the water for Kannon's bath, getting their jammies and diapers ready, I realized I couldn't really change her diaper and let him play in the tub by himself. So I turned to Kins and said, "Maybe Daddy can change your poopy, Sis." Jeff then got frustrated and said, "You've been saying you'd do it this whole time." So I took her into the bathroom, changed her diaper, and gave Kannon his bath, the whole while steaming with anger.

How could he not have changed her diaper? Didn't he see that I needed help? He's probably just sitting on the couch enjoying himself as I do everything. Jeff could tell I was upset, but I just told him I needed some time to think for a bit.

Finally, after the kids' bedtime routines, I could think through why that made me so upset. And I realized it wasn't Jeff's fault at all (although he admitted later on that he could have helped more), but rather it was my lack of communication. Instead of expecting Jeff to know what I needed and come to my rescue, I needed to ask him. Yes, I had been telling Kins I'd change her for last 15 minutes, and yes, I was the one trying to do too much. When I finally realized it, I passively asked Jeff in front of Kins, instead of looking at him and saying, "Hey Babe, I know I told her I'd change her, but it's kind of tricky now with Kannon's bath water running. Would you be able to help me by doing it this time?" I should have admitted my need for help and asked him straight forward.

It's not always about miscommunication though. It can also be about the lack of communication. Not stating your hopes or expectations or what you have on the calendar for the week. Not telling him how you're really doing, and asking for a break or some intentional time together. Jeff and I have learned the beauty and importance of being proactive in our communication. We are still growing at it, but we try to have one night a week where we sit down and talk about the upcoming week—what we have going on, projects we need to do, things we'd like to accomplish, appointments, schedules with the kids, date nights, getting together with others. Since we both work from need to. You can never over communicate! This planning doesn't mean that it protects us from any misunderstandings or arguments, but it does set us up for success and help.

In additional to trying to communicate well, another thing we do together is our marriage journal. Our friends Jeremy and Audrey Roloff have a marriage ministry Beating50percent, where they talk about the importance of spending time with our spouse once a week and asking the following questions:

1.   What has brought you joy this week?
2.   What's been hard this week?
3.   Is there anything that's gone unsaid or unconfessed?
4.   Are there any dreams or thoughts that have been running through your head all week?
5.   How can I pray for you this week?
6.   How can I serve you this week?

We have found these simple questions to transform our weeks. I love getting to have this intentional time with Jeff, whether it is 15 minutes after the kids go down for bed, or an hour long conversation during a date. We get to know each other's hearts, struggles, and joys and we get practical ways of how to pray for and serve one another. Sometimes I'm not so sure how to pray for Jeff, or while I do a lot to serve him, it may not be the thing that he needs the most. This practice has also allowed for things to be dealt with and not go unsaid to cause bitterness or resentment. You can go through these questions with your own journal, or check out their website where they have their

However you go about it, don't give up communicating with your spouse. Keep being intentional. Plan special time with just the two of you to have heart-to-heart conversations. Ask how he's doing. Tell him how you are really doing. Share your dreams, hopes, and longings. Friendship is the foundation for your relationship, so focus on continuing to grow and nurture that.

No one knows what it means to be intimate anymore and not just in our sexuality but platonically speaking as well. It's why whenever I'm out with friends and there's an awkward silence, we pull out the phone. We look down. We don't know what it means to be known anymore. In fact, I think we are terrified of being known, not realizing that's exactly where joy is hiding.

GUIDEBOOK

Communication

"LET YOUR "YES" MEAN "YES," AND YOUR "NO" MEAN "NO.""

Matthew 5:37 (CSB)

Sometimes the most profound truths are the most obvious. Jesus' simple command 2000 years ago is just as countercultural and challenging today:

Say what you mean. Do what you say.

Jesus is saying that if you have to add all kinds of promises or conditions to convince someone to believe you, then your words don't mean very much. The issue isn't whether or not it's OK to "swear" or to take oaths. The point Jesus is making is that character matters. Your words, your attitude, and your actions should all be sending the same message. People should know that you always keep your word.

The saying "actions speak louder than words" doesn't mean that words don't matter. It means that they only matter if you also do what you say. There's another Christian cliché that sounds similar: "Preach the gospel at all times and, when necessary, use words." The point, I think, is that everything we do communicates what we believe. It's not enough to say you love Jesus, if you don't act like it. It's not enough to say you love your husband, if you don't act like it.

But in your effort to remember that actions speak loudly, don't forget that the Good News of Jesus absolutely requires using our words. It's good news, right? Not just a good attitude. Following Jesus and sharing the gospel is about a lot more than just being nice.

In the same way, loving your husband is about a lot more than being nice. You have to show him, tell him, talk to him, listen to him, spend time with him, pay attention to him ... you get the idea.

Write your favorite quote,
song lyric, or Bible verse
related to the power of
words or connecting with
people in a meaningful way.
Draw a picture. Or write
a poem or song
this week, expressing
yourself creatively.

There are a lot of ways to communicate. All of them are important. All of them should echo the same message, like different instruments playing in harmony to create one song. And your song will be stuck in his head on repeat—hopefully, it's a love song that he sings without even realizing it while he goes throughout his busy day. Your song should make him dance. Your song should make him smile. Your song should give him comfort.

- **Do you and your husband have "a song"? What is it? What other song or song title would be a good summary of your relationship?**

_____

_____

_____

_____

_____

- **What makes that song, uniquely special? Is it the lyrics? Is it a memory associated with the song? Is it the mood of the music?**

_____

_____

_____

_____

_____

- If you were to create a playlist for your life together, what songs would you add to the mix? What songs would he add?

_____   _____

_____   _____

_____   _____

_____   _____

_____   _____

- Music is just one way people creatively connect with one another.

_____

_____

_____

- How do you best express yourself?

_____

_____

_____

- What kinds of things do you do to let your husband know that you love him?

_____

_____

_____

- **How does your husband express himself?**

_____

_____

_____

Now here's the key. Do you express yourselves in the same way? If not, you may think you're communicating with your husband and letting him know that you love you him, and he may think he's communicating with you, but it's like you're speaking different languages.

You know those embarrassingly awkward moments when someone can't speak a foreign language so they just speak louder? They may even speak slower or with an accent, like somehow being loud and slow and using a bad accent is going to help someone suddenly understand a different language. It's ridiculous and possibly offensive.

That's what it's like sometimes in marriage. A spouse can get frustrated and feel neglected or misunderstood. No matter how hard they try, things only get more awkward or tense as both people stubbornly continue to repeat their own ways of doing things. Don't be that girl. Learn what is meaningful to him and start speaking his language.

You've already seen that trust is vital for healthy relationships. Communication is a major part of developing trust and intimacy. Your husband has to know that when you say something, you mean it. He also has to believe that when he says something, you get it. He needs you to not only hear him, but to also understand him. You're listening. Real communication is happening, not just talk. No agenda. No saying one thing and meaning another. No guessing games.

Do you ever feel misunderstood?	YES | NO
Do you ever have trouble understanding your husband?	YES | NO
Do you always say what you mean?	YES | NO
Do you always do what you say?	YES | NO
Do you actually listen?	YES | NO

While we're on the subject of sending and receiving mixed signals, let's think about some other ways we communicate. Think back to the relationship between your actions and our words. All of these things are important in communicating well.

· What you say.
· When and where you say it.
· Why you say it.
· How you say it.
· What you do about it.

Do this quick exercise to think about how the truth can be clearly communicated or get lost in translation.

Your husband comes home after a bad day, but he doesn't want to talk about it. You've had a tough day too, but really want to talk about it. Give an example in each of these categories of the right and wrong way to communicate.

COMMUNICATION	GOOD	BAD
WORDS		
TIMING		
INTENT		
TONE		
BODY LANGUAGE		
ACTIONS		

The goal of communication should be connection. Communication should build trust and intimacy. It's about the other person as much as or more than it is about you. Be intentional this week to pay attention to how you interact with your husband. Make sure you're not sending mixed messages with the different ways you communicate. This is essential to not only the rest of this workbook, but more important, to the rest of your relationship. Be sure that he knows you love him.

Remember to give all of your attention to each other but you may want your phone to get started this time. That's up to you. You may normally have music playing in the background or you may not. This week it could be fun to have some music. Whatever you do, take clear action to demonstrate your love for one another by prioritizing this time together. If playing music, let it enhance the experience, not distract from it.

- Sit together on the couch or at the table. Start by comparing the playlists you created in the workbook. Compile your choices into an actual playlist and tell each other why you chose each specific song. If you have a favorite song together from your wedding or that has special meaning, take a few minutes to listen to it together.

- Go through the questions and exercises in the workbook, asking each other about how to best communicate. Be eager to listen. Don't be critical but be honest about what is most meaningful to you and lets you know that you're being understood and that you're loved.

- Read the words of Jesus and the Proverb, sharing how each of those verses helped you think about healthy communication.

- Ask each other about any of the other things you read and wrote about in the "on your own" section on the previous pages. Remember, this is a conversation with your husband. Enjoy it!

- Go to *Love That Lasts* in your library at *bethkeworkshops.com* and watch this week's video: Communication with Jeff and Shaunti Feldhahn. They are experts in the field of relational communication and have a particular gift for using data and analysis to help us all better communicate. After watching, ask each other what was most interesting, most challenging, and a big takeaway from the video. Use the video sidebar to take notes and to help your conversation.

- Pray together.

Communication with

Jeff & Shaunti Feldhahn

This section is a place to take notes if you also purchased the 12 corresponding video sessions from our 12 mentors. What did they say that resonated with you? What was your favorite part? What was most challenging?

The one who guards his mouth and tongue keeps himself out of trouble.

Proverbs 21:23 (CSB)

If you don't have this video
you can purchase it at

lovethatlasts.co/videoseries

Jeff & Shaunti Feldhahn
ON COMMUNICATION

Conflict

04

Whatever you may call it—a fight, an argument, a disagreement, a kerfuffle—it's bound to happen in your relationship. They come in all different shapes and sizes and at unexpected times (usually right before you're getting ready to head out to meet friends for dinner) and are never invited. No matter how long you've been married, how long you've been walking with Jesus, you can't avoid conflict because the truth is, two becoming one is really hard. Both of you have different ideas, opinions, personalities, proclivities, preferences, temperaments, and we're all sinners and can say things we don't mean in the heat of the moment.

I personally hate conflict. If conflict were a person on Facebook, I'd not only unfriend him, but I'd report him. In conflict, we either run from it and do everything in our power to avoid it, or we go head on and fight our way through it. I am a fleer (obviously) and Jeff is a fighter.

Jeff was my first boyfriend, and the first time we dated (because we broke up, then dated again before getting engaged), it was mostly all long distance. I had a lot of ideals of how relationships should look, and one of them was no conflict. I thought a healthy relationship meant you don't fight—or talk about things that bother you. Because we were dating long distance, I didn't want the little time we had on the phone, or the short time we actually had in person, to be filled with drama. I just wanted it to all be sunny and bright. That, however, led to a lot of misunderstanding and prevented us from getting to know each other on a whole other level.

Whenever Jeff said something that I didn't quite understand and was hurtful, I just swept it under the rug, not wanting to tell him how that actually hurt. I wanted to appear as the perfect girlfriend and I had this idea in my head that guys didn't like girls who are emotional or complain. So when I broke up with him, part of the reason was because I didn't think he really liked me, not nearly as much as I liked him. I didn't understand why he did the things he did—why he didn't come see me at work and hang out with me all day when he flew 2,000 miles to spend a week with me (I had a lot of ideals and expectations for him to live up to), why he avoided any conversation about the vision of our relationship, why he was silent at certain times that I wanted to have a heartfelt conversation. And each one of these things slowly hurt me and ate away at me. But instead of bringing them up when they happened and talking through it, I just let it go and, unfortunately, it brought our relationship to an end.

When we dated the second time around, I had grown a lot and realized that any healthy relationship has conflict and it's okay. Granted, it's never fun and never comfortable, but it's a part of being in a relationship and if it's handled well, can lead to further intimacy and growth. I was then able to tell Jeff about questions or doubts I had, to confess to him when he said something and it hurt me. And every time we had a hard conversation, I came away loving him more. I realized through those conversations that he really cared for my heart and I could be honest with him.

Fast forward to marriage, and I feel like our "conversations" have become much more heated. While we have had fights over big things like sex and Jeff's job and my anxiety and parenting, we usually fight over much smaller things, like taking out the trash and giving our kids baths and making the bed. When I look back on them, I tear up because of my sin and anger and harsh words in the moment. Somehow spouses can bring out the ugliest part in us. There have been times when I almost have an out of body experience and am left thinking, "What in the world? I don't even know this person. It's like I've been transported to my 13-year-old self with no self-control, whose emotions are flying off the wall."

The good part though is that it can get better! When you're walking with Jesus, filled with His Spirit, He changes you and grows you both as a couple. Jeff and I still fight, but we've gained some tools over the years to help us have healthy conflict—most of the time. Here are four things that have helped us:

1. **Don't yell or raise your voice.** When you're in an argument, especially one that hits both of your trigger points, most likely you will want to yell or raise your voice. And with that, you'll want to hurl hurtful words. It kind of goes hand in hand. We've tried to just make it a rule to not yell or raise our voice at each other. There's no need for it, and in doing so it kind of keeps the argument at bay. We're able to have more self-control and think about our words and listen to each other. Most likely you'll be angry, and that's okay, but it's trying to have self-control over that anger so it doesn't produce more sin. This is just a good rule to follow.

2. **Keep the small things small and the big things big.** Our really good friends have been married 11 years, and I remember one night at dinner they were talking about their drive over and how the wife brought up a small thing to her husband of something that had bothered her all day. But as the husband told the story, he was full of thankfulness and peace because he said she brought it up with such kindness and kept it small.

She then turned to us and said, "I've learned in marriage to keep the small things small and the big things big. So when he does something that is small, I don't blow up about it or let it bubble up all day to then explode that night when he does it again. I try to bring it up softly and talk through it. And when I do that, he's not on immediate defense mode, but can look at it with a clear eye and we can talk about it." Often in marriages, our arguments are over the small things that somehow blow up. But if we keep them small, bringing them up with a controlled spirit in kindness, it goes way better and remains small.

3. Take a timeout. Because I need to be by myself to process things and understand how I really feel and why I feel it, and because he gets so heated in the moment, we've learned to take timeouts during our longer arguments. When we usually have argued for a while and seem to just be saying the same thing over and over and neither one of us are understanding the other or humbly asking for forgiveness, we take a timeout. And we give it a time limit. For instance I'll say, "I need a time out. Give me ten minutes to think and we can come back and talk about it." Then we go into our different rooms and usually I cry a bucket of tears, and then when we come back together, we have clarity over the conversation. Now I'm not saying things I don't mean. I understand why I feel the way I do and can better explain myself to Jeff. I also can see how I was wrong and where I need to ask for forgiveness. And same goes for Jeff. We come back much more calm and able to actually talk through the situation.

4. Call an older couple. Sometimes you'll have an argument that neither of you can agree on. During these times, it's good to have a more experienced couple that you've both previously agreed on to go to. You want a couple who is for the both of you, won't take sides, has been married for awhile, and whom you both respect. If there's an issue that keeps coming up, then meet up with them and explain the issue at hand. Sometimes you need wisdom and counsel and another set of ears to walk through a hot topic.

When we were doing our premarital counseling, our mentors shared the verse for their marriage: "Do nothing out of selfish ambition or vain conceit. Rather, in humility value others above yourselves, not looking to your own interests but each of you to the interests of the others" (Philippians 2:3-4 NIV). Seek the Lord, and as you continue to, He'll help you to be humble and consider your husband's interests above your own (and vice versa). Conflict gives us the opportunity to step back and see how we can grow and become one on whatever topic it is.

Write a powerful quote, song lyric, or Bible verse related to conflict. Draw a picture depicting the essence of conflict. You may want to journal your thoughts on a significant conflict that is burdening you of the effects of unresolved conflict in general.

Conflict

04

"THEN PETER CAME TO HIM AND ASKED, "LORD, HOW OFTEN SHOULD I FORGIVE SOMEONE WHO SINS AGAINST ME? SEVEN TIMES?"

"NO, NOT SEVEN TIMES," JESUS REPLIED, "BUT SEVENTY TIMES SEVEN!"

Matthew 18:21-22 (NLT)

Conflict is inevitable. Let's just get the obvious out of the way. It's going to happen. Just like trust is built on little things and big things, conflict is going to happen in little things and big things. Let's commit to learning how to deal with conflict in the little things so that it doesn't escalate into something bigger. And whether we like to admit it or not, there will be times when we face more significant disagreements in marriage.

You may think that in a perfect world, we'd all just get along, but think about it: You saw the first husband and wife, Adam and Eve, blame each other for their disobedience to God in Genesis 3. Then you see their kids get into such a fight that one literally kills the other in Genesis 4. If Adam and Eve had conflict in a perfect world, then you and your wife and family members are going to have conflict. Until the new heaven and earth, where there will be no more pain, injustice, and death, we have to learn how to learn how to navigate conflict in a godly way.

In the Gospel of Matthew, Jesus' disciples asked him how to handle broken relationships. When people hurt us, how many chances do we give them before we walk away? How long should we put up with stubborn and selfish people? When do we say, *Enough is enough?*

Peter probably thought that his seven chances for serious offenses were generous. Symbolically, seven was a holy number of completion. Forgiving someone seven times may not have been a literal limit, but even if it was, the question for a specific could lead to a rigid and legalistic view of relationships. You can't plug relationships into a formula. There's no one-size-fits-all fit for everyone.

Jesus then says to take what we think would be godly and generous and then multiply that number exponentially. If seven times feels extremely gracious, multiply seven by another seven and then add a zero!

(Please note that forgiveness does not mean staying in an abusive or unhealthy situation. In that case, get help! The point is to focus on your own heart of forgiveness rather than on another person's actions.)

Even if we're on board with the whole forgiving thing, dealing with conflict in the first place may be difficult. We still need to learn to navigate the inevitably rough waters in order to make the journey as smooth as possible as a couple, as a family, as church members, as good neighbors, and in general as a human being in this world.

First, deal with conflict right away. Now, if you need to calm down for a minute, don't mistake this advice for saying something you'll regret by blowing up, but take a step back, catch your breath, and talk about whatever has upset you. You may actually be surprised at how many times what you're getting mad about is a misunderstanding and breakdown in communication.

But even if it leads to a tough conversation or an argument, the first step in learning to handle conflict is to stop putting things off and pretending like they don't bother you. You aren't helping anyone if you allow anger and unforgiveness to build up over time. Even if the conflict and offenses aren't big, the more you start to collect and the longer you carry them, the more they'll weigh you down and rob you of a joy and freedom as you walk with people through the days, weeks, months, and years. Even one tiny little pebble, when it gets in your shoe, can grow from an irritation to a serious problem. If you've ever gone to the beach then you know that a tiny bit of sand in your shorts can ruin a great day if you don't shake it out!

One of the most practical verses in the Bible as far as conflict and healthy relationships is Ephesians 4:26: "Do not let the sun go down while you are still angry" (NIV). Like the "seventy times seven" verse, this may be figurative or it may be literal. When possible, it's a great practice in your marriage to take this at face value and promise your husband that the two of you will never end the day fighting with unresolved conflict. Don't get in bed with your backs turned in anger. Don't settle for the habit of storming out and refusing to sleep in the same room. This communicates an unwillingness to be joined together as one. In general, seek a resolution as soon as possible.

How many days last week did you literally go to sleep with something seriously bothering you?

1 · 2 · 3 · 4 · 5 · 6 · 7

Would any of those things fall into the "angry about it" category   **YES | NO**

If you can identify specific things that have upset you recently and are still unresolved, write them down here.

_____

_____

_____

_____

_____

_____

Pay attention this week to the things that upset you and how you dealt with it.

MY WEEK

SUNDAY	MONDAY	TUESDAY
1	2	3

WEDNESDAY	THURSDAY	FRIDAY	SATURDAY
4	5	6	7

If you don't learn to deal with things quickly, you're choosing to allow conflict to pile up like rocks over what the Bible calls a *root of bitterness*. Since the beginning of time, our job has been to garden, to cultivate, and to flourish. The surest way to poison a relationship, including your marriage, is to slowly neglect a root of bitterness that needs to be pulled.

But don't just deal with them quickly; deal with them proportionately. Not all issues are the same. They all need dealt with, but not in the same way. Remember to address little things in little ways and big things in big ways.

You don't need to draw a line in the sand over how to load the dishwasher. You don't need to lose sleep coming to a resolution over how your shirts are folded or maybe not even always over how a careless word was more hurtful than intended. Mention it. Talk about it. But don't blow it out of proportion.

But sometimes there's a conflict that is really upsetting or where you are clearly on two opposite sides of an issue, like how to educate your kids or whether or not you'll even have kids, or what kind of home you'll move into, or how much travel is ok with your job. Sometimes the careless words or a pattern of thoughtlessness is worth losing sleep over so that the sun doesn't go down on what has become true hurt or anger.

A gentle answer turns away wrath, but a harsh word stirs up anger.
Proverbs 15:1 (NIV)

Write down a pet peeve or a personal preference that causes small degrees of tension (even if the conflict remains bottled up and never expressed).

_____

_____

_____

On a scale of 1 to 10, 1 = personal preference, 10 = I seriously can't live like this, how would you rate the issue?

1 · 2 · 3 · 4 · 5 · 6 · 7

YES | NO

Think about conflicts of various sizes. Is your reaction and method of addressing the issue typically proportional to its severity?

Circle your answer. I tend to: **OVERREACT | UNDERREACT**

Why do you sometimes overreact, exaggerating or fixating on conflict?

_____

_____

_____

Why do you sometimes underreact, minimizing or denying conflict?

_____

_____

_____

_____

_____

Right after the Bible says not to let the sun go down on your anger, it continues with "and do not give the devil a foothold" (Ephesians 4:27 NIV). Conflict that you don't shake out and put down become footholds for bitterness, doubt, jealousy, and all kinds of sin that calluses your heart until it is hardened toward that person—and eventually toward others too.

Eugene Peterson does a beautiful job in _The Message_ of summarizing Jesus' teaching on addressing problems from Matthew 18:15-17: "If a fellow believer hurts you, go and tell him—work it out between the two of you. If he listens, you've made a friend. If he won't listen, take one or two others along so that the presence of witnesses will keep things honest, and try again. If he still won't listen, tell the church. If he won't listen to the church, you'll have to start over from scratch, confront him with the need for repentance, and offer again God's forgiving love."

This is commonly referred to as a Christian model of conflict resolution or of church discipline. Specifically, Jesus is addressing how to confront sin, but the pattern of conflict resolution applies:

1. One on one

2. With trusted friends

3. Get help from your church

4. Repeat

Here's the summary:

- If there's something that's bothering you, talk about it. Don't let it fester. Do it quickly but proportionately.

- If it bothers you to the point of being angry about it, don't go to sleep angry. Talk about it as soon as possible in an effort to find a grace-filled understanding.

- Talk one-on-one first. In your marriage, go straight to your husband, not to your friends. Keep in mind the principles of trust and communication. You love each other. Be humble. Assume the best. Desire understanding. Give grace.

- If something is a major problem, seek the counsel of a few trusted friends. But don't skip straight to this step. Develop a habit of talking one-on-one first.

- If you've been talking to each other and you've sought the counsel of trusted friends, but you still can't seem to find a healthy resolution, seek out the help of your church—pastors, counselors, or specialized ministries.

God designed you for relationships. Conflict is inevitable, but when you develop a habit of honest and humble communication out of a desire to love one another well, you'll cast of a huge burden and experience the joy of loving and forgiving, being loved and being forgiven, growing and flourishing together. For better and for worse and for better again.

Remember to give all of your attention to each other. Turn off or put down your phones. Don't miss this week's video. It's 20 minutes of expert advice in the truest sense of the word. It's literally sitting down in the kitchen with Drs. Les and Leslie Parrott--both who are bestselling psychologists and marriage counselors. Imagine what their conversations and arguments must be like!

By the way, Drs. Les and Leslie Parrott are the brilliant couple who put together the assessment you did as a couple. So you are already more familiar with their insightful ministry than you may have realized.

The *On Your Own* section was a little bit longer this time. Conflict by definition is harder to talk about, so enter this time joyfully and prayerfully.

- Sit together on the couch or at the table. Start in prayer, thanking God for His love for you and for the love you share for one another as a couple.
- Ask the following questions:
  - What are some little things that we did differently and had to learn compromise and how to talk about those differences when we got married?
  - What funny quirks do I have that are part of who I am?
  - What habits or tendencies of mine have we learned to talk about as being unhelpful or hurtful?
  - When have we had to deal with a serious conflict with one another? It if escalated to a fight, what led to fighting and how have we learned from it?
  - When have we had to help one another deal with conflict outside of our marriage? For example, a bad work situation, trouble with a

neighbor, or extended family drama. What steps did you take and what was the outcome? Do you think you dealt with it the right way?

- Read the words of Jesus and the proverb, sharing how each of those verses helped you think about a healthy perspective on conflict resolution.

- Ask each other about any of the other things you read and wrote about in the "on your own" section on the previous pages. Remember, this is a *conversation* with your husband, not a list of problems. The goal is to identify way you can love and serve one another, recognizing potential conflict and learning how to address them early and lovingly so that things don't escalate into fights or bitterness. The goal is seriousness but the conversation shouldn't necessarily be heavy.

  - Compare your thoughts and examples on the scale of *little* and *big* things. Did you have similar perspectives? Were there any major differences between what you consider a little or big deal?

  - Look at the calendar you kept and talk honestly about things you wrestled with this week. How can you help one another in those areas specifically?

  - Commit to the steps summarized at the end of the *On Your Own* portion of the section: deal immediately and proportionately, don't go to sleep angry, talk one-on-one first, then seek trusted counsel, finally seek help from your church pastors and ministries if a conflict ever gets to that point.

- Go to *Love That Lasts* in your library at *bethkeworkshops.com* and watch this week's video: Conflict with Les and Leslie Parrott. Then, ask each other what was most interesting, most challenging, and a big takeaway from the video. Use the video sidebar to take notes and to help your conversation.

- Pray together.

Conflict with

Les and Leslie Parrott

This section is a place to take notes if you also purchased the 12 corresponding video sessions from our 12 mentors. What did they say that resonated with you? What was your favorite part? What was most challenging?

_____

_____

_____

_____

_____

_____

_____

_____

_____

_____

_____

_____

_____

If you don't have this video
you can purchase it at

lovethatlasts.co/videoseries

Faith

05

One of my friends' got married when she was young. She had always longed to be married and be a mom, and when she went to college she met a guy, fell in love, and was married a year later. She's still married now, nine years later, and has two beautiful children, but it's been a grueling road that now tells a beautiful redemption story.

When they got married, she knew a lot about her husband, but one thing she wasn't so sure about was his walk with the Lord. He said he recently came to know the Lord and was following Him, but after marrying him, it became apparent that perhaps he hadn't truly given full control of his life over to the Lord. Behind closed doors she saw how anger had a stronghold on him. There was still a lot of healing he needed to walk through, things in his life he still needed to surrender and trust the Lord in. Marriage quickly became very difficult.

When they had gotten married, she was so in love, but knew in the back of her head that perhaps this wasn't the best timing, but she went ahead anyway. Some friends and family mentioned concerns or some red flags they saw and told her to wait, but she dismissed those because she wanted to be married so badly. Soon after getting married, it became a real struggle when they wouldn't agree on things, or share the same values. She wanted him to lead her, to pray for her, and talk about the Bible, but he didn't do those things. He would go to church, but that was about it. And his anger problem became a huge issue. She became the spiritual leader in their home and felt alone a lot of the times. She would pray and pray for him and their marriage, but felt as if God wasn't listening, like nothing was changing.

Years later they went through a particular hard time and decided to separate for a while. Through that separation, they both sought counsel from an older couple at church, and things started to change. For the first time, he really trusted and respected the older mentor and was open to counsel. The Lord grabbed hold of his heart, and soon began to change areas in his life. He confessed his anger problems to the Lord, and although it's still a battle, the Lord is changing him and giving him victory. She learned to how to better love and serve him, all the while finding her true identity and security in the Lord.

Her faith has grown exponentially, being encouraged to continue to pray for him, regardless of how "fast" her prayers are answered. She knows the Lord hears her and is at work, and has a high calling to lift her husband up in prayer constantly. Now their marriage is better than it ever has been. They are walking with Jesus together, serving the church together, and being the hands and feet of Jesus in their home through foster care. They counsel other marriages in their church, ones that are in the same hardship that they once were in.

I love how their story is a redemption story. How he changed, and how she continued to love him through it all, and learned to love in truth and courage. To do the hard things at time, like be separated, so things could actually change.

Growing up my friends and I heard in youth group how important it was to not date or marry someone who wasn't a believer. We prayed for our future husbands and held out hope of what kind of man God was going to bring us. As life went on, however, the waiting grew longer, the "pickings" seemed to be slim, and the more bad relationships they had that led to hurt and confusion, led way to letting this truth slide "just a bit."

It's not so much about marrying someone who says they're a Christian or someone who goes to church. But rather, do they love Jesus and follow Him? Do they spend time with Him and read His word? Do they talk about Him, or what they're learning? Are they open to correction and counsel? Do they seek wisdom and are full of the Spirit? They aren't going to perfect, of course, as we certainly are not! But are they growing? Do you see significant fruit? Can they lead you spiritually?

And of course, as you look for a man with those qualities, look at your own life. Are you following Jesus? Are you in His word, surrounded by other believers, seeking mentors, and being full of the Spirit? Be who you want to attract.

For those who are already married, hopefully you are married to someone who is truly walking with the Lord. This will affect your vision for your family, the purpose of your marriage, what priorities you set up, and how you deal with conflict. Because two key elements of any marriage is grace and forgiveness, and if you don't have Jesus, it would be really hard!

God has put you two together to grow both of you and cause you to become your best selves. You need your spouse to do that as God intended. You both are called to pray for each other, shepherd one another's hearts, encourage each other to grow and share truth with one another. And as you continue to learn your passions and callings, find out ways of how to do them together. How can you be a team, to go out and glorify God together? So how can you grow your faith together?

1. Pray for your husband. This is the highest calling you have as a wife. God is the one who knows your husband's heart better than you, and who can change him. Commit to praying for him daily, praying for his heart, character, job, how to lead you and your family, wisdom in decisions, etc. The Lord hears your prayers and is at work in his life.

2. Shepherd one another's hearts. This will look differently for each couple. Regardless of how it looks though, we are called to encourage and speak truth into each other's lives. Share what God is teaching you, what you're reading or listening to, talk about scripture and sermons and values. Ask him how his heart is, what he's been thinking about lately, what's weighing him down, how you can pray and serve him. And when you see an area in his life that needs to change, gently and kindly tell him. Pray through how to go about it, and that he'd have a heart of humility to receive your words. And likewise, be open to his advice to you as well.

3. What is God calling you to as a couple, or family? What gifts and callings and passions do you all have? How can you make God known, and be his hands and feet, together as a couple? Do you love babies and want to serve in the nursery at church together? Do you want to open your home to foster care or those without father figures? Do you want to start a Bible study together or mentor a younger couple? Do you want to hand out lunches to the homeless once a month or disciple high schoolers? What can you do together? Because marriage doesn't end with us, it's about being on mission together, and that brings the most joy.

Finally, if you're married and your husband doesn't know Jesus, don't give up hope. This was not God's Plan B for you, but it was God's best. You are called to love and respect your husband and are his biggest way of seeing Jesus. How can you respect him, care for him, and love him? How can you shine your light in your home? Even if you don't see a change, don't lose hope. Continue to entrust your husband to the Lord.

We don't want spouses to be our "everything." We want spouses who actually love Jesus more than they love us. When Jesus is your "everything," you are actually freed up to love the other person better. With more freedom and actually out of true love, because you don't need something in return. You're loving them because Jesus has loved you.

Faith

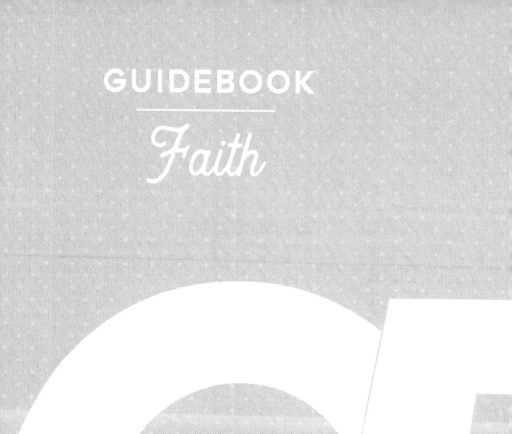

"TEACHER, WHICH COMMAND IN THE LAW IS THE GREATEST?" [JESUS] SAID TO HIM, "LOVE THE LORD YOUR GOD WITH ALL YOUR HEART, WITH ALL YOUR SOUL, AND WITH ALL YOUR MIND. THIS IS THE GREATEST AND MOST IMPORTANT COMMAND. THE SECOND IS LIKE IT: LOVE YOUR NEIGHBOR AS YOURSELF. ALL THE LAW AND THE PROPHETS DEPEND ON THESE TWO COMMANDS."

Matthew 22:36-40 (CSB)

Jesus said that God's will for our entire lives could be summed up in loving God above anything or anyone else, and then loving others as if their needs were your own. This summarizes the Christian faith. He said that everything written in the Old Testament—all the rules, instructions, prophetic corrections and promises—all of it ultimately boils down to truly loving God and loving one another.

It's that simple, but we know our own hearts and that the simplicity doesn't mean it's easy. In fact, as you've been digging into these last topics of trust, communication, and conflict, relationships are hard work. There's nothing more satisfying than a right relationship with God and with others, especially in marriage, but there's nothing that requires more intentionality.

In his book *For the Love,* D. A. Carson put our need for intentionality this way: "People do not drift toward holiness." Think about how true that is in your own experience. He goes on to explain: "Apart from grace-driven effort, people do not gravitate toward godliness, prayer, obedience to Scripture, faith, and delight in the Lord."

Living near the beach, it's easy to see the tides change and the rhythms in nature. But you don't have to stand on the shore to see this simple truth. Look up at the sky. Even on a still day, if you watch long enough, you begin to see the slow movement and changing shapes of the clouds as they drift through the sky.

Everything is moving. The question for you is whether or not you are moving closer to God, growing deeper in your faith, or are you drifting away from Him. If you aren't paying attention or intentionally focusing your heart on God, then you will be pushed along by the changing tides and shifting winds of each day. You'll drift away.

This reality of naturally drifting away and never drifting toward is true in your love for God and for one another in marriage (or any relationship). Jesus is clear that when your love for God is a priority, then your relationships can take their rightful place and shape. When our love for God and for one another is pure, then we'll find that Scripture and all that it reveals about abundant and eternal life finds new clarity and meaning. Faith moves from our heads, to our hearts, spilling out into our relationships and into everything we do.

What things do you naturally find yourself drifting toward—what consumes your thoughts, emotions, motivations, and activities?

_____

_____

_____

_____

When do you feel your thoughts, feelings, and activities most prone to drift away from faith in God?

_____

_____

_____

Think about the specific language used to describe the ways you should love God and people.

What does it mean and what does it look like to *Love the Lord your God with all your heart, with all your soul, and with all your mind?*

_____

_____

_____

_____

What does it mean and what does it look like to *Love your neighbor as yourself?*

_____

_____

_____

As water reflects the face,
so one's life reflects the heart.
Proverbs 27:19

Write a favorite quote, song lyric, or Bible verse related to faith or belief. Draw a picture of a vine. Write about the first time you began to understand what faith in God truly meant.

Jesus uses a beautiful picture of this organic connection in our relationships with God and with each other. Look at how he explained faith and love to his disciples.

> I am the vine; you are the branches. The one who remains in me and I in him produces much fruit, because you can do nothing without me.
>
> As the Father has loved me, I have also loved you. Remain in my love. If you keep my commands you will remain in my love, just as I have kept my Father's commands and remain in his love.
>
> I have told you these things so that my joy may be in you and your joy may be complete. This is my command: Love one another as I have loved you.
>
> John 15:5, 9-12 (CSB)

The disciple who wrote down these words, John, was practically obsessed with love. It was a healthy obsession. In fact, he refers to himself in his Gospel as "the disciple Jesus loved." This wasn't an arrogant nickname, suggesting that Jesus loved him more than the other disciples. It's a testimony to the reality that John's life was so transformed by his relationship with Jesus that his entire identity could be summed up by the fact that Jesus loved him.

In the verses you just read, Jesus is teaching his disciples that every good thing in their life will grow out of their relationship with God. Their lives are to be defined by love for God and for one another. Literally nothing that is truly good is possible apart from his blessings. God is good. God is love. Loving God and loving one another are inseparable; you can't do one without the other (1 John 4:8). A vine is the source of life for branches. Branches can't live and bear fruit without the vine. Jesus is saying that it's impossible to experience abundant life, joy, satisfaction, and true love without being deeply rooted in and dependent on God's love to flow through you.

Faith in God means trusting that he is everything we need for joy and satisfaction in life. Obedience to God is an act of love. It's a way of saying, "I believe that you always know what is best for me." God's commands are an expression of his love for his children. Your heavenly Father loves you. Jesus loves you. What could possibly be better than that? Let this

	SUNDAY	MONDAY	TUESDAY
YOU	1	2	3
YOUR HUSBAND			

truth change your life so completely that it flows into your relationships, bearing good fruit for the whole world to "taste and see that the Lord is good" (Psalm 34:8).

We'll look at several different rhythms in life that focus our hearts on the love of God later in this workbook, so for now let's start with the simple definition of faith of loving God and loving one another, using the points that were introduced in reading.

Pray for your husband.

Write down a specific topic of prayer each day this week related to how you want God to draw you and your husband deeper into relationship with him.

WEDNESDAY	THURSDAY	FRIDAY	SATURDAY
	5	6	7

Shepherd one another's hearts. What is God teaching you right now that you can share with your husband?

_____

_____

_____

_____

How can you encourage or help your husband with Christlike love?

_____

_____

_____

_____

_____

How can he encourage you?

_____

_____

_____

What is God calling you to as a couple, or family?

_____

_____

_____

What opportunities do you have to encourage other people—neighbors, coworkers, friends, church, community—to grow in their faith?

_____

_____

_____

How are you involved in your church, connected to other branches in the vine?

_____

_____

_____

If you're not currently involved in a church, what church would you like to visit?

_____

_____

_____

Remember to give all of your attention to each other. Turn off or put down your phones. This week's video is the shortest in the series, only 15 minutes, but it is packed with wisdom from an incredible couple talking about faith in God and God's faithfulness to us.

(Side note: One of the ways that the church pastored by one of this week's featured video mentors seeks to help people grow in their faith is with The Bible App and The Bible App for Kids by YouVersion.)

- Sit together on the couch or at the table. Start in prayer, thanking God for His love for you and for the love you share for one another as a couple.
- If you did the creative option of a quote, picture, or journal, share that with each other.
- Read the words of Jesus and the proverb, sharing how each of those verses helped you think about your faith.
- Ask each other about any of the other things you read and wrote about in the "on your own" section on the previous pages.
- Go to *Love That Lasts* in your library at *bethkeworkshops.com* and watch this week's video: Faith with Craig & Amy Groeschel. Then, ask each other what was most interesting, most challenging, and a big takeaway from the video. Use the video sidebar to take notes and to help your conversation.

Faith with

Craig & Amy Groeschel

This section is a place to take notes if you also purchased the 12 corresponding video sessions from our 12 mentors. What did they say that resonated with you? What was your favorite part? What was most challenging?

_____

_____

_____

_____

_____

_____

_____

_____

_____

_____

_____

_____

_____

If you don't have this video
you can purchase it at

lovethatlasts.co/videoseries

Calling and
Purpose

06

C.S. Lewis once said, "Friendship ... is born at the moment when one man says to another, 'What! You too?'" When I look at all of my close friendships over the years, this quote perfectly sums up the moment we became besties. Whether it's over a favorite book, what we love to do, or a particular struggle we have, when we realize that we are the same on something, it's like this immediate connection.

When I was single, I so longed to be pursued by a man and get married. It seems so easy and normal, and yet there were no guys knocking on my door—or at least ones that the feelings were mutual. It was so hard to wait, and although I lived my life, I went to bed a lot of nights feeling lonely and longing for my deep desire to be married to finally be fulfilled. One of my mentors told me one day that I need to keep walking forward, living my life and following the Lord and His adventure for me. "Just keep going, Alyssa. One day, you'll look to the side of you and see that there's a man running right alongside you who is going in the same direction, and your paths will meet and then you'll know. That's who God wants you to run the rest of your race with. You'll be better together than apart. But until then, just keep going." I didn't need to waste time, or not live my life or sit and twiddle my thumbs waiting for my man to show up. I could run free and fast and enjoy all that God had for me in that season of singleness.

I had graduated college in California and had accepted an internship in Hawaii to disciple high school girls at a church there. The two weeks before I flew across the ocean, I drove back home to Washington to spend time with my family and go to a friend's wedding. I was excited for this next adventure God had for me; it really was a dream come true and a huge answer to prayer. Then out of the blue I hear about how this guy named

Jeff wanted to meet me and then started pursuing me. This guy caught my eye (and heart). Then a week later, I flew across the ocean and he went down to Oregon to finish two years of college.

It certainly didn't seem like we were going in the same direction. We were 2,000 miles apart and in two completely different seasons of life. He was in college and I was in a full time job. I was in a season where I could marry quickly if I met the right guy, and he needed years until he was fully ready to support and lead a wife. However, our interests, passions and convictions were the same. I remember so many conversations on the phone where I would just sit on my couch and my jaw would drop because I couldn't believe he thought that too. He loved Jesus like no guy I had ever met, loved reading and studying His word and could talk about it for hours (which I loved), and yet he would have so many insights that I never would have thought of. He loved High School Musical, which at the time was my current favorite.

As Jeff and I continued to date, then break up, and date again, our hearts continued to be on beat with each other, and as we grew and life happened, our dreams and visions for our lives became the same and we knew that we didn't want to live another day without having each other in it. We knew that God had brought us together to keep running this race together. And we truly were better together than apart. Which becomes more and more apparent to me as the years go by. I'm so thankful for the way Jeff has poured into my life and helped me to see things in a new and different light. He encourages my weaknesses, cheers me on in my strengths and makes me laugh the whole way through.

When we got married, we had the same convictions and a solid foundation of Jesus and His word. We loved making Jesus known in unique ways, pouring into college age students, and having people over. We wanted to travel and see the world, loved to read, and one day wanted to have a big family. The first year of marriage, we traveled like crazy for Jeff's job. He spoke all over the world, and going into marriage knowing his speaking schedule, I had quit my job so I could travel with him. I went through a real identity crisis our first year of marriage though. I had worked since I could remember to save up for dreams I wanted to accomplish. I was always in ministry and unfortunately had found a lot of my worth from my performance. With two words, "I do," my life completely changed. I became a wife, stayed at home, and had married someone who was asked to speak everywhere. I loved that God had given Jeff a platform to make Him known, but sometimes it was hard when we were somewhere and I seemed invisible. People didn't want to see me; they only wanted to meet Jeff. Which I totally get, but it caused me to really dig in and see what God said about me and where my true identity came from. During that year, I started to blog just to tell the funny stories that happened to me as a "rookie wife." I realized how therapeutic writing was for me, and suddenly I realized that I could pour into people through written word. And I could do it on the road. And so Jeff and I continued this rhythm for quite some time: We traveled, he spoke, and I wrote.

Then when our daughter was born, things had to change. We still traveled, but I couldn't keep the pace that Jeff went. Kins and I stayed home a lot, and I found myself feeling lonely and abandoned. Sometimes I believed the lie that Jeff loved work more than me. I was anxious all the time, never quite knowing how often Jeff would be gone that month. It seemed like he was doing his thing, and I was left at home. While this may work for many families, it didn't for us and I felt like I was crumbling and we couldn't understand each other. He didn't understand why it stressed me out, or why I didn't want to go on some trips. This was a dream for him, and such a blessing that we could travel and share about Jesus. I loved that he did it, but didn't understand why it was so hard for me. It just felt off for us. And it was a constant fight.

As I shared earlier , we finally came to our mentors and shared about this constant argument we were having and they really helped us work through it. I understood myself more and why I felt so anxious. They gave me tools to work through that anxiousness, and at the same time helped us to come up with a game plan. The husband spoke on the phone directly to Jeff: "Jeff, now that you're married your ministry is not just about you. It's not 'single Jeff' anymore, but rather it's you and Alyssa. God gave you to each other, so how can you both do ministry together. It's going to look differently now and you have to consider one another." It was life changing for us.

When you get married, your ministry and job is not just about you anymore, but it's about you together. How can you do this life together? God's given each of you different giftings, but one calling. It needs both of you. So how can you work together? What is He calling you to together? It's going to look differently for every couple, because everyone is different. There's no right or wrong, and it can change and morph during different seasons. And then when you start having kids, it becomes about your family, not just you as a couple. What is God calling your family to? He's given each of your kids different personalities and giftings that your family needs; your family isn't complete without that little one. Now you're called on mission as a family.

For us, in this season, Jeff decided to not travel nearly as much. He goes about every quarter now, and usually only when we can all go as a family. He tries to do as much as he can from home, and we've started to do a lot of projects together. I love working alongside Jeff. We love being at home with our kids and I know it's a huge blessing that Jeff is home during the day and we can co-parent together.

I know our lifestyle will look differently ten years from now, but regardless of what we're doing or how we're doing it, we're convinced we'll do it as a family, together.

This is a huge topic that may take a long time to work through as a couple. You may need to talk through it with a mentor couple too. Talk about your passions, giftings, what you want to be doing and how it affects each other and your family. How can you make God known together? What is God calling your family to?

Write a favorite quote, song lyric, or Bible verse related to purpose. For this week's artistic option, draw either something to represent what you believe to be your ultimate purpose, what the next step of faith may be, or how you feel trying to figure out God's purpose for your life.

Calling and Purpose

"AS JESUS WALKED BESIDE THE SEA OF GALILEE, HE SAW SIMON AND HIS BROTHER ANDREW CASTING A NET INTO THE LAKE, FOR THEY WERE FISHERMEN. "COME, FOLLOW ME," JESUS SAID, "AND I WILL SEND YOU OUT TO FISH FOR PEOPLE." AT ONCE THEY LEFT THEIR NETS AND FOLLOWED HIM."

Mark 1:16-18 (NIV)

Simon and Andrew weren't just spending a weekend on the lake, fishing with their buddies. Fishing was the family business, their career. Then Jesus completely turned their world upside down and gave them a brand new purpose and meaning to what they already knew how to do. Jesus spoke to them in a way that they understood and called them in the middle of their normal, everyday life. Immediately Simon and Andrew dropped what they were doing in order to experience what Jesus had in store for their lives.

The same was true for James and John whom Jesus would call in the next verses—the same John who wrote the famous Gospel of John, 1-3 John, and the Book of Revelation! Those books are possibly the most beautiful and awe-inspiring literature in the New Testament.

There are a few of things to notice in these verses:

- When Jesus called them, He didn't give them all of the details.
- Even though they weren't expecting it, they followed His calling immediately, believing that He was worth any change of plans or personal sacrifice.
- Jesus' purpose for their lives expanded on what they already knew and were good at, but He did something that they never would have imagined.

These three things are true about God's purpose for your life too. He is calling you into relationship with Him and there is absolutely no way to know exactly what all He has in store for you as you follow Him in faith. But you can know for sure that it will be worth it.

Here's something else to consider: Simon and Andrew, James and John, and any of the other disciples may not have even realized when they dropped those nets that this was the first step of faith that would change the rest of their lives. Chances are, they didn't understand in that moment that they would have to make some decisions about the fishing business and how it fit into their lives as followers of Jesus. They just knew that in that moment, they wanted to follow him. And the next day they would essentially make that decision again. And again. And again. And three years later, as Jesus was hanging on a cross, they didn't fully understand what was happening. Surely their minds raced back to all of the decisions they had made and the conversations they had with family and friends and coworkers, explaining that they were going to follow Jesus.

Had they been crazy? Did they make a terrible decision? Did they completely misunderstand what Jesus wanted them to do?

After Jesus was resurrected, the disciples were found fishing (see John 21). Jesus is once again standing on the beach calling out to His disciples, asking about the day's catch. When Simon Peter realizes that it's Jesus, he dives in the water, fully clothed, and swims back to Jesus. John and the other disciples row back and meet him. It's actually pretty comical. But the Bible shows us over and over that God calls ordinary people for his extraordinary purpose.

While everyone won't be called to leave their professions in order to go into "career ministry" jobs, God's purpose for each of our lives is to follow Jesus. This is ultimately an application of what it means to "love God and love people" in your own life and sphere of influence. As Colossians 3:17 puts it, "Whatever you do, in word or deed, do everything in the name of the Lord Jesus, giving thanks to God the Father through him" (ESV).

1. How would you define the purpose of life in general?

_____

_____

_____

_____

_____

_____

2. What would you say is your purpose in life as a follower of Jesus?

_____

_____

_____

_____

_____

_____

3. What are your specific talents and God-given abilities?

_____

_____

_____

_____

_____

_____

4. How would you describe your personality?

_____

_____

_____

_____

_____

5. What are your interests, hobbies, and passions?

_____

_____

_____

_____

_____

6. If you could do anything in the world with your life, what would it be?

_____

_____

_____

_____

_____

_____

7. What experiences in your past have shaped who you are today?

_____

_____

_____

_____

_____

8. How do those things identified above fit into current opportunities?

_____

_____

_____

_____

_____

9. What would it look like to use your abilities, passions, dreams, and opportunities to better love God, to love others, and to help others enter into and grow in a relationship with Jesus?

_____

_____

_____

_____

_____

_____

10. What are your husband's natural abilities and unique gifts?

_____

_____

_____

_____

_____

11. How would you describe his personality?

_____

_____

_____

_____

_____

12. What are his interests, hobbies, and passions?

_____

_____

_____

_____

_____

_____

13. If he could do anything in the world with his life, what do you think it would be?

_____

_____

_____

_____

14. What experiences in her past have shaped who he is today?

_____

_____

_____

_____

15. How have you seen God working in him and through him?

_____

_____

_____

_____

_____

_____

16. What is something special about how he shows the love of Christ to people that he may not know about himself?

_____

_____

_____

_____

17. When you consider all of these things about your life and about his, what might God want to do through your life together?

_____

_____

_____

_____

_____

18. How can you encourage him in his unique opportunities?

_____

_____

_____

_____

_____

19. How can he encourage you in your unique opportunities?

_____

_____

_____

_____

_____

20. Even if you don't know what you're called to when it comes to some big special purpose, what step of faith can you take as a couple or as a family to experience God and to share His love with others?

_____

_____

_____

_____

Remember to give all of your attention to each other. Turn off or put down your phones. This week may take more time to discuss the questions, Scriptures, and video, so be sure to plan accordingly. The video is only 20 minutes and it's a fantastic resource on how two unique callings in life can work together in a beautiful way as a couple.

- Sit together on the couch or at the table. Start in prayer, thanking God that He has a plan for your lives as individuals and as a couple or family. Ask God to begin making his purpose for your lives clear and to give you the confidence to step out in faith, one step at a time.
- If you did the creative option of a quote, picture, or journal, share that with each other.
- Read the words of Jesus and the proverb, sharing how each of those verses helped you think about your faith.
- Walk through each of the 20 questions you did on your own, comparing your answers. Don't stress. It's not about quizzing each other to get the right answers. This is an awesome way to get to know your husband in a deeper and more intimate way.
- Note: Your questions 1-9 will line up with his 10-19. Question 20 is your answer as a couple.
- Go to *Love That Lasts* in your library at *bethkeworkshops.com* and watch this week's video: Purpose with Zac and Jennie Allen. Then, ask each other what was most interesting, most challenging, and a big takeaway from the video. Use the video sidebar to take notes and to help your conversation.

Purpose with
Zac & Jennie Allen

This section is a place to take notes if you also purchased the
12 corresponding video sessions from our 12 mentors. What did
they say that resonated with you? What was your favorite part?
What was most challenging?

Trust in the Lord with all your
heart and lean not on your
own understanding; in all your
ways submit to him, and he
will make your paths straight.

Proverbs 3:5-6 (NIV)

If you don't have this video
you can purchase it at

lovethatlasts.co/videoseries

Zac & Jennie Allen

Sex

Jeff and I come from two completely different spectrums when it comes to sex. I grew up in a church that taught that sex should only be in marriage and was part of the "purity ring" culture. Jeff, on the other hand, let MTV and the locker room teach him about sex. Jeff was my first boyfriend, and he started dating at 16. He had had multiple partners before we got married, and I was a virgin. Even though I was so excited to have sex with the one man I committed myself to, I still had misunderstandings of sex that still have ramifications to this day. No matter what your history is, we all have some baggage to unpack and heal from when it comes to sex.

We live in a sex-crazed culture where we can't go grocery shopping, open our computer, click on our facebook app without hearing about or seeing sex. Regardless of how hard you fight against impurity, some misconstrued thoughts are bound to seep into your mind and affect your marriage. And that's not even considering your past or your husband's. The hurt you may have gone through, the shame, regret, thoughts that taunt you when you least expect them.

Whatever you story is as a couple, there is hope and healing. And God has put the both of you together to continue the healing process in each of your lives. The thing is, sex was God's idea and it is so good. To think that God made it and gave us body parts that are meant only for pleasure is crazy to me. He intended sex to be an act where you and your husband are drawn closer together, where you are completely naked in front of each other—physically and emotionally—and completely loved and accepted. You are completely known and loved in that moment, in marriage. It's a picture of how God loves us, of how He sees us as we are, and loves us completely and abundantly.

Author Timothy Keller said that sex is the renewal of our vows. Every time we have sex with our husband, we are reenacting our vows made to another on the altar. You're remembering your covenant, and acting out your promise to one another. To choose the other, serve the other, cherish the other.

Before we got married, we read *Intended for Pleasure,* a book explaining sex, and how it works and ways to overcome some obstacles that may come up in sex. I enjoyed it, but since it was written from a doctor, it was more black and white. I got the impression that if you do exactly as they said, then it'll be awesome every time. When we got married, however, sex wasn't as easy as I thought it would be. I realized it's a whole lot more about your mind and hearts than I had ever expected. It's not just about doing certain things physically, but it's about the heart behind sex. The why. What you think about as you're doing it. I learned that it was all about giving and serving, not about what I can get out of it. I learned that sex can usually be the pulse of the relationship. Are you loving and serving one another, or being selfish and distracted? Sex is a lot more like a dance, then a science chart.

Jeff and I have grown a lot in sex. We've had to work through him not desiring it because of an overloaded work schedule, me not desiring it during some parts of my pregnancies and being a new mom. We've had to communicate a ton about expectations and desires. Of lies and memories. We've had to give a lot of grace. And at the same time, we've laughed a lot. Sometimes sex is like a gourmet dinner and sometimes it's like drive-thru. I can say that as the years go on, it gets better and better. It's so good, and I can't wait to see where we're at twenty years from now.

Here are a few things that have helped Jeff and I learn to serve one another more in sex:

1. Sex is about serving, not taking. Of course the hope is that you'd enjoy it too, but go into sex thinking of how you can serve him. And when you focus on serving him, you'll end up enjoying it more than ever. For sex to be at the level God created it to be, it comes down to both of you finding ways to serve each other, not take what you can. Think about what he likes. Ask him. And go for it. Even when you're tired or want to be served, focus on what you can do to please him. And when both of you are looking to serve the other, that's when sex is amazing.

2. Talk about expectations. Sometimes the fights or hurt can be caused because we each had different expectations. He thought you guys were going to have sex tonight, but you had just finished telling him about how hard your day was and only want to take a bath and go to sleep. Set yourselves up for success by talking about how often you'd both like to have sex. At the beginning of the week, talk about what you have going on so you're both aware of your schedules and what your week will look like. Ask how you're doing serving him in this area? What can you do better? Where can you grow? Are you both pursuing each other, or does it seem like one of you is always asking? Figure out a good rhythm for the both of you. I know after we had our second baby, I was so exhausted all the time, I never thought of having sex. As unromantic as it was, I told Jeff I needed to plan out when we'd have sex for this small season. It'd help me to plan ahead. If I could plan it out, I could better prioritize him and us. And in so doing, it helped me to be more spontaneous when those times came too.

3. Pursue sex with your husband. The first year of marriage, this was not a problem for me! But then when kids came along, sex took a backseat. Suddenly I was consumed with diapers and exhausted from late nights, that I couldn't think of putting on a pretty piece of lingerie and have sex. If I had a spare 30 minutes, I wanted to be sleeping! This greatly hurt Jeff. I realized how I needed to prioritize sex because not only was it important to us, but it also showed Jeff that he was important and a priority to me. I'll admit that most of the time, this doesn't come naturally to me (thanks, hormones), so I have to work at thinking about and planning for sex. I need more time to warm up, to think about Jeff throughout the day and think about sex. It helps if I make it special, buy a new piece of lingerie, or serve something easy for dinner so I won't be so tired that night when I hop into bed with my hubby. Sex is important and beautiful. Figure out how you can make it a priority.

4. Guard your mind. I'm realizing more and more that what I let into my mind, what I watch and listen to and believe, really affects our sex. If I have a misconception about something, it stops me from fully enjoying sex, or feeling guilty. If my mind wanders as we're doing it, then I lose the point—to enjoy my husband and serve him. Sex is an opportunity to revel in God's goodness, to serve and love your husband, and to be with him and only him. It's the one time that no one else or nothing else has your attention. Just your husband. So focus on him. Think about the qualities you love about him and are thankful for. Pray for him. Enjoy him.

GUIDEBOOK

Sex

05

66[JESUS] ANSWERED, "HAVEN'T YOU READ IN YOUR BIBLE THAT THE CREATOR ORIGINALLY MADE MAN AND WOMAN FOR EACH OTHER, MALE AND FEMALE? AND BECAUSE OF THIS, A MAN LEAVES FATHER AND MOTHER AND IS FIRMLY BONDED TO HIS WIFE, BECOMING ONE FLESH—NO LONGER TWO BODIES BUT ONE. BECAUSE GOD CREATED THIS ORGANIC UNION OF THE TWO SEXES, NO ONE SHOULD DESECRATE HIS ART BY CUTTING THEM APART.99

Matthew 19:4-6 (MSG)

You're not having déjà vu. You read a different translation of these verses in the first session, *Theology of Marriage*. But it's important to catch something that may not be obvious, especially if you're familiar with the "two shall become one" language of marriage.

This may not exactly be the illustration you were hoping for in a chapter about sex, stay with me. Imagine a political debate or talk show where someone is trying to back someone else into a corner with a polarizing question that can only be answered in a way that offends one side of an issue or the other. Even worse, if the person tries to dodge the question by not answering it, he loses credibility with both sides. It's a lose-lose-lose situation. This is exactly what it was happening when the religious leaders of Jesus' day attempt to trap him with a question about whether or not it's ever okay to get a divorce.

Of course Jesus' answer is brilliant. He doesn't answer or avoid their question. He swings the spotlight back over onto his opponents, asking them whether or not they understand one of the most elementary yet profound truths in Scripture. This is *Bible 101: Introduction to God and Humankind.* Jesus basically says, "Before we talk about ending a marriage, let's be sure that everyone here understands the mind-blowingly beautiful miracle that God did with creation and continues to do in marriage. Did you guys somehow skip the first pages of your Bibles? You really should go back and read them. Seriously. It's fantastic stuff."

Eugene Peterson's paraphrase of the Bible does a beautiful job of highlighting the fact that spirituality and sexuality are intertwined in marriage. This is why God is so clear throughout Scripture that sex and marriage should be treasured as uniquely beautiful gifts. Sex in marriage is a masterpiece by our

Creator. Taking sex outside of its perfectly designed context, making it an act of the self rather than of union, or anything that desecrates the sacred marriage covenant is like taking scissors to a priceless work of art.

Look at these phrases describing marriage:

> ... *made man and woman for each other* ...
> ... *firmly bonded to his wife, becoming one flesh*
> —*no longer two bodies but one* ...
> ... *this organic union of the two sexes* ...

Don't dismiss this language as purely symbolic and poetic. Yes, there is a theological and metaphorical significance to two becoming one, but it's also a very literal and sexual union of two bodies becoming one flesh—one man and one woman.

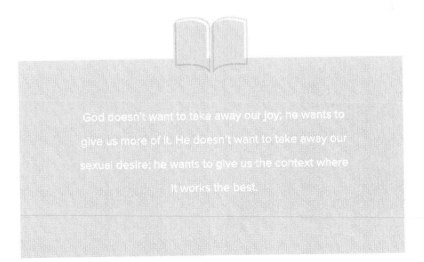

God doesn't want to take away our joy; he wants to give us more of it. He doesn't want to take away our sexual desire; he wants to give us the context where it works the best.

Sex was God's idea. It's a really good idea! Christians often have the mistaken belief that sex is taboo and dirty. This is not only a mistake, but it's a harmful distortion of this amazing gift. But for a long time, the Church found it easiest just to tell kids that it was bad and not do it until you get married. Talk about whiplash!

Sin has hijacked one of God's greatest gifts. Sexual desire for and pleasure in your spouse has always been part of the way God made men and women.

When did you first learn about sex?

_____

_____

_____

What was your earliest understanding of sex?

_____

_____

_____

How did friends, family, and the culture influence your view of sex?

_____

_____

_____

How did the Church, the Bible, or Christians influence your view of sex?

_____

_____

_____

Have you ever talked about any sexual background with your husband?

_____

_____

_____

Do you talk openly about sex with your husband now—what you like, what he likes, etc.?

_____

_____

_____

On a scale of 1-10 (1 = all about me, 10 = all about her) how would you rate your view of sex? (Not rating your view on how good sex is, but on whether or not your focus is honestly more on you or him.)

1 · 2 · 3 · 4 · 5 · 6 · 7 · 8 · 9 · 10

All about me   *All about him*

> *Look back at the verses Jesus was quoting earlier.*
>
> *So the Lord God caused a deep sleep to come over the man, and he*
> *slept. God took one of his ribs and closed the flesh at that place. Then*
> *the Lord God made the rib he had taken from the man into a woman*
> *and brought her to the man. And the man said:*
>
> *This one, at last, is bone of my bone*
> *and flesh of my flesh;*
> *this one will be called "woman,"*
> *for she was taken from man.*
>
> *This is why a man leaves his father and mother and bonds with his*
> *wife, and they become one flesh. Both the man and his wife were*
> *naked, yet felt no shame.*
>
> *Genesis 2:21-25 (CSB)*

You see this picture of an intimate moment where God creates woman and presents her to the man. It's like a wedding where the bride is given to the groom. And look at the first thing Adam does when he sees Eve for the first time. He starts singing a love song! And the chapter closes as if the curtain was being drawn for the honeymoon as they were naked and felt no shame—only knowing the kind of joy that caused spontaneous singing.

That's the kind of sex and nakedness and intimacy between a husband and a wife that God has created for you. This doesn't necessarily mean that you should sing next time you see your husband, but you can certainly declare your love for and admiration of him, thanking God for his kindness to you in blessing you with your marriage.

Get creative and do something fun or romantic to surprise your husband. It doesn't have to be a crazy-elaborate gesture, it may be as simple as surprising him at work, leaving notes, or a favorite meal.

Share a picture of you and your husband on snapchat, facebook, twitter, or whatever your social media of choice happens to be. Thank God for your husband and expressing your love for him. We'd love to see these too, so if you want to spread the love with everyone else, don't forget to use the hashtag #LoveThatLasts.

Write a favorite quote, song lyric, or Bible verse related to desire for your wife. For this week's creative option, think about a song that is romantic or sexy. You may even want to add to the previous playlist you created or create a new playlist for your own mood music.

Remember to give all of your attention to each other. Turn off or put down your phones. Hopefully, giving each other should be extra enjoyable this week. In fact, you may want to plan for either a longer date night tonight or possibly split this up into two times together because the video this week is 45 minutes. Craig and Jeanette provide one of the most candid conversations about a healthy sex life. Seriously, when was the last time sex positions were discussed in a Bible study? But don't freak out (or get overly excited): it's not a how-to guide to Christian sex.

While it may not feel all that romantic to take notes, you're going to want to pay attention to their wisdom when it comes to expectations, communication, etc. The goal is to help you see sex clearly as God created it—and to fully enjoy one another!

- Sit together on the couch or at the table. Start in prayer, thanking God for the intimacy he has created you to share with one another—spiritually, emotionally, and sexually. Ask him to draw you closer to one another in every way and to bless your marriage.
- Read the words of Jesus and the proverb, sharing how each of those verses helped you think about sex.
- Ask and share about anything from anything else from the *On Your Own* section or the personal reading.
- Go to *Love That Lasts* in your library at *bethkeworkshops.com* and watch this week's video: Sex with Craig and Jeanette Gross. Then, ask each other what was most interesting, most challenging, and a big takeaway from the video. Use the video sidebar to take notes and to help your conversation.

- If this hasn't been a date night the past several times (or whatever time of the day you may be meeting), make it a special time. You may want to have some food or snacks and something to drink.

- Share memories from your wedding night and honeymoon. If you have pictures of the honeymoon, look at those together like you did with the wedding pictures during the first session.

  - What were you thinking and feeling that first night we were married?

  - What are your favorite memories from the honeymoon?

  - What were you most excited about? Nervous about?

  - Was anything surprising, or did anything funny happen?

  - Do you remember anything funny happening while having sex?

  - What are some of the best times you've had sex? What made those experiences especially good?

  - What do you not like? What do you really like? What would you like?

If you did the creative option of choosing a song or making a playlist, play the music and tell your husband why you chose that first song. What about it makes you think of him?

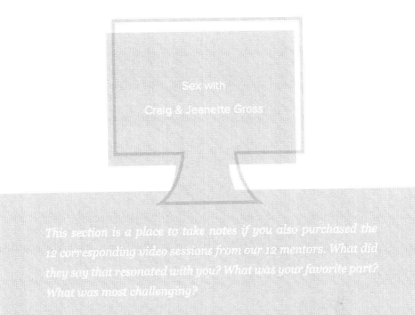

Sex with

Craig & Jeanette Gross

This section is a place to take notes if you also purchased the 12 corresponding video sessions from our 12 mentors. What did they say that resonated with you? What was your favorite part? What was most challenging?

_____

_____

_____

_____

_____

_____

_____

_____

_____

_____

_____

_____

_____

Let your fountain be blessed, and rejoice in the wife of your youth, a lovely deer, a graceful doe. Let her breasts fill you at all times with delight; be intoxicated always in her love.

Proverbs 5:18-19

If you don't have this video
you can purchase it at:

lovethatlasts.co/videoseries

Craig & Jeanette Gross

Parenting

08

When Jeff and I got married, we knew we wanted kids one day, and probably a whole team of them. We were excited to become parents—one day. We were on the 3-5 year track plan. The first year of marriage we were traveling multiple times every month, leading a college ministry, got a dog (which is almost like a newborn!), each wrote a book, and were learning how in the world to be married! We were full, enjoying every moment and excited to be on this adventure.

It seems like as soon as you get married, everyone asks, "So, when are you planning to have kids?" Hello. We literally just got married yesterday. (I mean, Jeff's mom, bless her heart, was so excited for us to get married that when we were engaged, she asked this question. She was dying to be a grandma!)

And then it happened. We had one "oopsie" moment, and I was pregnant. Surprise! We had only been married 10 months. It's not that we weren't ready or excited, but it just came a lot sooner than we had planned. And I'm so glad it did. We were so excited to start this journey of parenting together, to raise a family, disciple our kids, and be a team. God knew the time we needed to become parents, and he knew the exact day Kinsley needed to be born. It was no mistake. She was born when she was for a purpose. Maybe it's so she'll have the friends that she'll have, or so she can be a light to someone in her exact grade. Whatever it may be, I'm so thankful we became parents earlier than planned.

Kins was two weeks late to the party. To say that I was ready to meet this little love and be her mommy was an understatement. When I heard the sweetest little cry, and a warm, precious baby girl was placed on my chest, I couldn't believe it. She had been inside of me. I had grown this child. God had given us this little girl. And she was perfect. I loved feeling her skin on mine. Holding her little hand, kissing her head. She immediately calmed the moment she was placed on my chest.

Becoming parents caused us to grow closer and sanctify us in a way that marriage couldn't. Marriage does take a lot of sacrifice and grows us immensely, but at the end of the day, you can kind of do your own thing. Parenting is a whole other animal. Suddenly there's a little person that depends on you for their *life*. Like literally, if you didn't care for them, they'd die.

The first year with Kins was the best. I treasured her and soaked up every moment. I couldn't believe God had given me a little girl. However, the first six months were hard on our marriage. Suddenly Jeff and I had all of these expectations that had never been spoken, and ones we never realized we had. Who would give baths? How many baths do you give a week? Who wakes up at night with her? Who changes the diapers? How do you bond with her? How do you be intentional with a baby? We were stretched, and found ourselves disagreeing often. I put a lot of pressure on Jeff, and at the same time, he'd tell you that he had a misconstrued vision of parenting. He came into it, not even realizing it, that we each had our different roles to play, and when we accomplished our roles, then we could rest. So for instance, he had his roles, and when he was done, then he was done for the day. He didn't want to help me if I wasn't done yet. Which caused a lot of tension between us because I was exhausted. I needed help, and even if I could do it, it was nice to have a break once in awhile.

It wasn't after we moved to Maui that things began to change. We started to meet with our mentors once in awhile to talk to them about how we were doing, and learn from them. As I mentioned before, they have five kids, so are basically sanseis when it comes to parenting! We longed to gain insight and wisdom of how to parent now, in the baby stage, and store up their nuggets for when Kins and any other kids we had grew up. As we began to meet with them, and get immersed in our community here that is full of other young families, Jeff's heart started to change. He does so much for us, and works so hard, but as the leader of our home, he's called to continue to serve and help our family even after a long day of work. That's not to say that he doesn't take breaks, or that I give him time to just rest, but now he jumps at any chance to help out. I can't believe I get to parent alongside this man. He is so helpful, thoughtful and amazes me with what he can handle.

We loved our little Kins so much that we decided to have another close together. And so I get pregnant with our second, and we had a sweet baby boy Kannon. They're 23 months apart, and Kannon was a much harder baby than Kins. Jeff was completely different this time around. He has the sweetest relationship with Kins, she is just a daddy's girl, and he did anything and everything to help with Kannon. I remember one morning in particular, it had been a long night, and I was in the living room with a crying baby and a crying toddler. I don't remember what had happened, but I remember thinking that if I didn't get a break I'd lose it. When Jeff came up the stairs and saw the look on my face, he told me to go and get a coffee and sit for awhile. He had this. He knew I needed to get out. And I actually took him up on it. Two hours later, I came back, and there was Jeff reading on the couch, Kins was quietly playing legos on the coffee table and Kannon was in his bouncer, chewing away. All was quiet. I couldn't believe it.

Jeff and I are still rookies when it comes to parenting, but there are some key things we have learned as we're in the trenches of having littles.

1. You need your kids and they need you. God has entrusted you with your children. It wasn't be mistake, but was made with great purpose. God knew that your kids, each one, needed to be in your family. Without them, it's not complete. They have unique giftings and strengths that all of you need. Your kids need your specific care, your specific calling and strengths and wisdom. And you need your kids specific personalities and hearts to not only grow you, but also bless you. Children truly are such a blessing from the Lord.

2. You and your husband are on the same team. Sometimes it can be easy to compare yourself with your husband. To make parenting a competition. "I took out the trash. He vacuumed. I changed a million poopy diapers today and he didn't. He took the kids to their lessons, I cooked." Sometimes I catch myself doing this, but it always leads to me being upset with Jeff. It's not a competition. You're not being judged by what you do, or who does more. You each are contributing to the family in different ways, and both are valuable. Sometimes, you'll carry more of the load, and other times he will. Remember that you are called to serve your husband and your family, and that's a gift. Give him grace; I'm sure he needs breaks! Give yourself breaks; you need them to! It's okay if the house isn't immaculate or if the laundry goes unfolded for a day (or three). Cheer each other on. Help one another and ask for help.

3. Take breaks. This is for dads and moms, but I think it's a lot harder for us moms to allow ourselves to take breaks. I feel like I'm just not learning to take breaks, but I still need to be proactive in it. It's a lot to be a mom!

It's nonstop. And although it's the greatest calling, you also need to take breaks to rest, refuel, and refresh. And when you do, you'll always be a better wife and mom. So think through what fills you up. What gives you life, refreshment? And then plan ahead to go and do that at least once a week. Plan it out with your husband, get a babysitter if you need to, or switch with a friend. Maybe it's going to get a coffee by yourself for an hour once a week, or going to a park to read, or taking a long run or going shopping with girlfriends. There's a planned break each week, and then give yourself little breaks each day. Maybe you need a nap when your kids nap, or enjoy taking baths after a long day, or wake up early to go for a walk before the kids wake up. Whatever it is, think about what you need to be the best mom that you can be.

4. Seek counsel. Parenting is no joke. It's not just about the sleep training, or potty training, or getting your child into the best school. It's all about their hearts and shepherding them. It's about showing them God's love, teaching them about His truth, educating them, allowing for opportunities to grow and fail, and letting them know that no matter what, they are immensely loved. Each child is so different, and each season has different beauties and different hardships. No parent is perfect, and we all need help. It is so important to find an older couple whom you and your husband respect and look up as parents. Get together with them once in awhile, facetime, or email. Ask them questions. Allow them to speak into your life. You need the encouragement, and the wisdom! Also, along these lines, good books can really encourage you as you parent too. Two of our favorites are *The Mission of Motherhood* by Sally Clarkson and *Never Say No* by Mark and Jan Foreman.

5. Pray. Pray, pray, pray. God knows your child's heart better than anyone else. He knows what they need, and you have full access to ask Him for wisdom and insight. I feel like 99 percent of the time I have no idea what I'm doing. I'm constantly on my knees asking the Lord for wisdom and insight into my children's hearts. And He gives it! He really does. Uplift your children to the Lord constantly, asking Him to draw them to Himself, to shape their hearts, to grow them in maturity and wisdom and discernment. Continue to give your heart, your desires and struggles to Him. He is your strength and song. As Isaiah 40:11 says, "He tends his flock like a shepherd: He gathers the lambs in his arms and carries them close to his heart; he gently leads those that have young" (NIV).

6. Remember that children are a blessing from the Lord. On the hard days, and the good days, children are the sweetest gift. They don't fulfill you or satisfy you. You can't find your identity in them or your sense of purpose; that only comes from God. But man, they are gifts! Sometimes I may be having a particular hard day, and Kins will come in the room wearing some way-too-small getup that's her brother's, and shouting in her "man voice" (thank you, Jeff!) saying, "Mama's a saint!" I can't help but laugh. She brings so much joy to our home!

Even though we don't realize it, having a loving and healthy marriage example in your parents has profound impact on you. Tens of thousands of micro moments and conversations and watching your mom and dad love and serve each other, amidst their problems and baggage, and all those other things, adds up over thousands of hours to show you what it takes. To show you what it looks like.

Write your favorite quote, song lyric, or Bible verse related to babies, kids, or growing up. If you're extra artistic, get creative with your handwriting or draw something to represent family.

GUIDEBOOK

Parenting

"THEN CHILDREN WERE BROUGHT TO HIM THAT HE MIGHT LAY HIS HANDS ON THEM AND PRAY. THE DISCIPLES REBUKED THE PEOPLE, BUT JESUS SAID, "LET THE LITTLE CHILDREN COME TO ME AND DO NOT HINDER THEM, FOR TO SUCH BELONGS THE KINGDOM OF HEAVEN."

Matthew 19:13-14

While the Old Testament has basically an entire book on parental advice (Proverbs), Jesus didn't speak much about parenting directly. He didn't have a wife and kids; yet as the only begotten Son of our heavenly Father, in whose image we are created, Christ shows us a holy heart full of patience, love, grace, and wisdom.

In the story you read above, parents were bringing their babies and children to Jesus. A common practice in that time was to have a holy man or rabbi bless your child. In fact, there are similar traditions today, but the point here isn't about whether or not you should have your child dedicated to the Lord in a church service. The point here is that Jesus made time for and valued these kids. Their hearts and lives were just as important as the grown men and women. He honored the parents and was gentle with the children. He even pointed to them as an example. We can learn three things from His example:

1. Kids are an invaluable blessing.

Whether you have your own or not, when are you prone to see kids as more of a burden than a blessing?

_____

_____

_____

If/when you have kids, what will you do to love them well?

_____

_____

_____

2. We can learn from children.

Look at the awe and wonder of children. What can you learn from their example?

_____

_____

_____

Next time you have to correct, discipline, or deal with something that you don't want to, stop and think about how it relates to your own relationship with God. But here's the great news: your heavenly Father is never too frustrated, busy, or tired for you. He always makes the right decisions, never loses his temper, and always invites you to spend time with him while he works.

What is something that you constantly say to or do for your kids?

_____

_____

_____

What does that teach you about God's love for you?

_____

_____

_____

_____

_____

3. It's our job to introduce them to Jesus.

How are you intentionally teaching your kids about God?

_____

_____

_____

Is there anything you are doing that could keep your child (or other people around you) from seeing the truth about why knowing Jesus really matters?

_____

_____

_____

Like is often the case, Jesus' words likely had literal meaning, "Let the kids come to me, the kingdom of God is for them too," and a symbolic meaning, "A relationship with God requires childlike faith." This doesn't mean naïve or immature and unquestioning; it means that we must be completely dependent upon our Father as children do for all of their needs and find joy in the good gifts He provides. Little kids just want to be in the presence of their parents. They want to see and learn and know that they are noticed and loved.

But it's easy to get impatient with kids or exhausted by their constant need for attention or supervision. So often we just want them to do what they're told. Why won't they listen? Why won't they do what they're told? Why don't they learn from their mistakes? Why do they keep doing that over and over? Don't they know that's bad for them or that they'll get hurt?

You can probably identify with this story, whether or not you have kids of your own. Look at the disciples. They're *rebuking* parents for bothering Jesus with their kids. They probably thought they were doing the important ministry of preaching and healing a favor. The disciples probably weren't being ugly, but *rebuked* is a strong word to indicate that there was zero patience for wasting time dealing with kids.

The same can be true in our culture, where it's sometimes seen as a "value" to be too busy with seemingly important things to recognize the gift of children.

The ultimate purpose of parenthood is to introduce children to Jesus so that they can grow up to love Him with all of their hearts, minds, souls, and all of their strength. Don't let other priorities get in the way.

ON YOUR OWN

You may or may not be a mom at this point. There are few topics as touchy as parenting. How will you educate, how many extracurricular activities can kids be involved in, how will you discipline, how much sleep should they get, how much screen time is okay, how much sugar is okay, and the list goes on and on. Everyone wants to do the best job possible.

But take a deep breath. Relax. Believe it or not, there's no one-size-fits-all guide to perfect parenting. There's no such thing as the right way for all Christian parents to educate or discipline their kids, for example. But you'll have personal convictions and discernment for what works in your home for each kid. Ultimately, you have to choose what fits into your purpose as a couple and as a family.

God has a plan and knows what he is doing. Whether through adoption, birth, or helping others in the church or community, you have the awesome privilege of loving on kids and helping them know Jesus.

Look back at what you identified as your personal calling and purpose as a couple or family. Write it down here.

_____

_____

What effect does your God-given purpose have on parenting decisions, including if, when, and how many kids you want to have?

_____

_____

Now let's do some general questions on hot topics to help you discuss some of the important with your husband.

1. How many kids would you like to have? _____

2. How would you describe your childhood?

_____

_____

3. What good things from your childhood do you want to pass on in your own family? What examples do you intend to follow?

_____

_____

_____

4. What do you want to avoid and not do as a parent that was a part of your own childhood?

_____

_____

_____

5. What forms of discipline do you think are effective? What is the purpose of discipline?

_____

_____

_____

6. Do you have an opinion on what type of education you prefer (public, private, home, other form of school)?

_____

_____

_____

7. How important is it to be active in a local church? What does it mean in your mind to be active in church?

_____

_____

_____

8. What excites you about kids?

_____

_____

9. What scares you about kids?

_____

_____

10. What specific things do you need prayer for as a wife or mother?

_____

_____

_____

For centuries, many Jewish families have affixed a little box or cylinder called a mezuzah to the doorways of their homes. A mezuzah contains a tiny scroll with the words of Deuteronomy 6:4-9 and 11:13-21, the passage of Scripture often referred to as the Shema, which is the first word in the original Hebrew language, meaning hear or listen.

This is a beautiful picture of family, parenting, and passing along your faith from one generation to the next. You'll see the mention of doorposts that these traditional Jewish families have taken literally. Read the first half of this Scripture and let it sink deep into your heart. You should also notice the familiar command that Jesus said is most important in life. This has been God's purpose for his people all along.

Listen, Israel: The Lord our God, the Lord is one. Love the Lord your God with all your heart, with all your soul, and with all your strength. These words that I am giving you today are to be in your heart. Repeat them to your children. Talk about them when you sit in your house and when you walk along the road, when you lie down and when you get up. Bind them as a sign on your hand and let them be a symbol on your forehead. Write them on the doorposts of your house and on your city gates.

Deuteronomy 6:4-9 (CSB)

You know the drill by now. Turn off or put down your phones. Give each other all of your attention. This week has another video that clocks in around 45 minutes with Willie Robertson and his wife, Korie, from *Duck Dynasty.* Their hearts for kids are bigger than his world famous beard!

- Sit together on the couch or at the table. Start by asking each other to name a favorite memory from your own childhood and what made it special.
- Ask one another the ten questions from the list of that can become potential areas of conflict if you don't have clear communication.
- Read the words of Jesus, the Shema, and the proverb, sharing how each of those verses helped you think about children and parenting.
- Ask each other about any of the other things you read and wrote about in the "on your own" section on the previous pages. Remember, this is a conversation with your husband. Enjoy it!
- Go to *Love That Lasts* in your library at *bethkeworkshops.com* and watch this week's video: Parenting with Korie and Willie Robertson. Then, ask each other what was most interesting, most challenging, and a big "takeaway" from the video. Use the video sidebar to take notes and to help your conversation.
- Now is a great time to reconnect with the mentor couple you may have identified in the first session. Invite them over or meet up to ask about parenting and anything that you've read, studied, and discussed since you last got together.

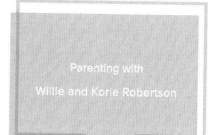

Parenting with

Willie and Korie Robertson

This section is a place to take notes if you also purchased the 12 corresponding video sessions from our 12 mentors. What did they say that resonated with you? What was your favorite part? What was most challenging?

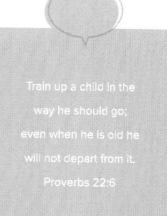

Train up a child in the
way he should go;
even when he is old he
will not depart from it.

Proverbs 22:6

If you don't have this video
you can purchase it at:

lovethatlasts.co/videoseries

Willie & Korie Robertson.
ON PARENTING

Money

99

Growing up my mom always did all of our finances. I remember every Saturday morning she would sit down to balance out her checkbook for the week with her calculator. (No, not on her phone. An actual calculator that went click, click, click when you put numbers in it and that you had to start over every time you pressed a wrong number.) I remember countless times going to the bank to deposit checks and countless conversations she had with my dad over how to spend their money each month. Should they spend this amount? They needed to take out this much to fix the dryer. And then save for family vacations every summer. Needless to say, when Jeff and I got married, I assumed that I would do all the finances. Not because I wanted to (Lord have mercy, numbers make my brain spin), but because I thought that was how it was done and because when Jeff and I talked about it during our pre-marital counseling, he said that would help him. So, I took on the responsibility.

About three months into our marriage though, I was drowning. Finances stressed me out like no other; however, since Jeff was working 60-hour weeks and I stayed at home, I thought I had to do the finances. I couldn't ask him to take this on too. I had the time, so I should figure it out. Plus, I was the saver, and he was the spender. I thought I needed to set the budget and only I could really be the one to stick to it.

Finally, Jeff found me crying one Saturday morning as I stared at the computer screen, trying to make sense of our bank account. I had no idea what I was doing and couldn't keep up. Since Jeff's job was unconventional, he had checks coming in from 10 different areas, all of which came sporadically. Then he had people he had to pay every month, but it all depended on how much they made each month, which was never the same. I couldn't keep up. Jeff sat down next to me at the table, and after I explained my frustrations with him, he totally got it. Since he was better with numbers than I was and he knew more about when and where the money was coming in and out, we realized that the finances needed to be his responsibility.

In marriage, you have to do what serves your marriage the best. It won't look like your parents' marriage, or anyone else's, because you are both unique in your giftings and callings. You have to figure out what roles best suit each of you and do whatever serves the other best. For us, Jeff doing the finances just made sense. Yes, it was one more thing for him to do, but he could do it so much better and faster than I ever could. I could serve him in a whole bunch of other ways, like laundry and cooking and gassing up the cars.

For us, we usually get big checks twice a year, instead of steady, more frequent ones, so we have to budget accordingly. Regardless of how your income works, or what your budget looks like, there are a few key factors when it comes to finances, in this order:

1. Tithe. Give generously.
2. Pay your bills.
3. Save.
4. And then spend however seems best for your family.

First, the Lord tells us to give generously with a cheerful heart. Tithe your money. Give it to people in need. Maybe that looks like giving a certain percentage to your church each month, buying a car seat for a mom in need, providing dinner for a family every week, or putting your money aside for when a big need arises like a friend's adoption or refugee help.

However it looks, make it a priority. There is so much joy when we give, and when you join in on the work God is doing across the world, or across your neighborhood. Second, everyone has bills, and although they're not fun, it's a fact of life. So pay them on time. Third, save. Have an emergency fund for when your car breaks down or your dishwasher leaks (because you know its going to happen), or set goals with your spouse of things you want to do. Places you want to see, experiences you want to have. Saving can make it happen. And then finally, spend. If you've done all that, then you're free to spend your money on whatever you may need or a possible want. That's the big picture. The small picture will look different for each couple. Maybe you set a strict budget, or maybe it's more loose. Maybe you pay your bills online where you schedule your bank to take out your money each pay period, or maybe you write checks for each bill. Maybe you save up for a down payment on a house, or for a special gift for your spouse's birthday. It'll look different for each couple, and in each season. Talk to your spouse about it, make a plan, and ask an older couple for guidance if you need to.

Finances are a big deal, and for most couples, it may be the thing that you butt heads on the most. It can cause a lot of stress and uncertainty. Trust is a big part of it—trusting your spouse and trusting the Lord who ultimately provides for our every need. But be diligent to not let money divide you. Let it be an opportunity to communicate and come on the same team. Jesus said in Matthew 6:21, "For where your treasure is, there your heart will be also." Money tells a lot of what you hold close and cherish. And in marriage, it can tell where you are going as a couple, what your goals are, what you're called to as a couple, and what you and your spouse are passionate about. So let money draw you and your spouse together, and allow you to have a vision for your future and a way for you to live out your passions.

GUIDEBOOK

Money

"DON'T STORE UP FOR YOURSELVES TREASURES ON EARTH, WHERE MOTH AND RUST DESTROY AND WHERE THIEVES BREAK IN AND STEAL. BUT STORE UP FOR YOURSELVES TREASURES IN HEAVEN, WHERE NEITHER MOTH NOR RUST DESTROYS, AND WHERE THIEVES DON'T BREAK IN AND STEAL. FOR WHERE YOUR TREASURE IS, THERE YOUR HEART WILL BE ALSO ... NO ONE CAN SERVE TWO MASTERS, SINCE EITHER HE WILL HATE ONE AND LOVE THE OTHER, OR HE WILL BE DEVOTED TO ONE AND DESPISE THE OTHER. YOU CANNOT SERVE BOTH GOD AND MONEY."

Matthew 6:19-21, 24 (CSB)

Notice that Jesus didn't say that you can't have both God and money. He doesn't even say that you can't *enjoy* both God and money. Jesus said that you can't serve both God and money. They can't both be your master, which is what the term *Lord* means. You have to choose one.

The master you work for and the treasure you are seeking are either temporal or eternal in nature. One can be taken and lost, but the other lasts forever. Jesus is asking you to choose which is better: heaven or earth, God or money. When we step back to see the full picture, it's easy to see which one is the better choice. But it's hard when we don't have the big picture in view. Or when we have bills due.

So ask yourself, where is your ultimate allegiance? What are you working for? And then keep your priorities in mind when it comes to creating, and sticking to, your budget together.

When you have a tough decision and it comes down to money or a sense of conviction, what do you do?

Pray about it:	first	during	after	never
Think about money:	first	during	after	never

How important is money to you?

1 · 2 · 3 · 4 · 5 · 6 · 7 · 8 · 9 · 10

Not at all   *It consumes me*

How important is God's purpose for you?

1 · 2 · 3 · 4 · 5 · 6 · 7 · 8 · 9 · 10

Not at all   *It consumes me*

What do the answers above reveal about your treasure and master?

_____

_____

If someone looked at your bank statements what would they most likely think (i.e. you eat out frequently, go shopping, give generously, etc)?

_____

_____

Based on the purpose you identified for your life in session 8, does the way you handle money reflect intentionality in pursuing your purpose?

_____

_____

What can you do to take steps toward handling your money more intentionally to pursue your purpose?

_____

_____

Storing up treasures in heaven doesn't simply mean that you refuse to be openly greedy or to engage in sketchy business practices; it means that your God-given purpose is the guiding principle for your life and decisions—including how you make, save, give, and spend money.

One thing you'll notice as you compare notes with your wife and if you watch the video is that there are often differences between marriages and also within marriages on attitudes toward money.

Most likely, there is a *spender* and a *saver* in your marriage; but it's also possible to have two *spenders* or two *savers* in a relationship.

I am a:	spender		saver
My husband is a:	spender		saver

What problems can arise if both people are *spenders?*

_____

_____

What problems can arise if both people are *savers?*

_____

_____

What problems can arise is one person is a *spender* and one is a *saver?*

_____

_____

In your own marriage, where do problems or conflicts about money arise?

_____

_____

How do you try to balance one another when it comes to money?

_____

_____

What do you enjoy spending money on?

_____

_____

What do you hate spending money on?

_____

_____

When do you get stressed about money?

_____

_____

How are you generous with your money?

_____

_____

It's helpful to consider how you grew up when trying to understand the way that you and your husband view money.

How would you describe your financial situation growing up?

1	2	3	4	5	6	7	8	9	10

Dirt poor   *Filthy rich*

Who worked:	dad	mom	kids
	step-dad	step-mom	other:

How often was money discussed in your home?

1	2	3	4	5	6	7	8	9	10

Never   *Nonstop*

How would you describe the general attitude toward money in your home growing up? What sort of money-related things were discussed?

_____

_____

Describe your expectation of what life would look like when it came to a home, car, income, vacation, shopping, social life, etc.?

_____

_____

_____

Are there any areas in your life where you intend to use your money differently than the way it was used in the home you grew up in? If so, what are they and why do you want to treat those things differently?

_____

_____

_____

_____

What is your most important financial priority?

_____

_____

Now you may or may not have a strict budget, depending on your sources of income and various obligations, but it's important to get at least a general picture of your money—where it comes from and where it goes.

The questions above will help you understand yourself and each other better when it comes to how you view money. Your conversation about those things will increase healthy communication and enable you to better navigate potential conflict—hopefully even avoid some conflict altogether!

This final activity will give you something to work with when you get together with your husband. This will be a very practical tool. Feel free to be as detailed as you want or need to be based on your personality and your financial realities. Under each category, you may want to get detail—breaking down housing, for example, into rent or mortgage, utilities, maintenance, etc. Or you may just want round numbers. Either way, make sure the numbers are realistic, even if not perfect. The key is to get at least a framework sketched out so that you and your husband can be on the same page.

HUSBAND'S INCOME	WIFE'S INCOME
TITHE / GIVING	SAVINGS
HOUSING	SPENDING
TRANSPORTATION	OTHER

You know the drill by now. Turn off or put down your phones. Give each other all of your attention. This week ...

- Sit together on the couch or at the table. Start by talking about some of the jobs you've worked. What did you want to be when you grew up? What was your first job? Worst job? Best job? Strangest or funniest thing to happen at work? Have you ever had any jobs you stayed in just because of the money? Or jobs you loved, but they made money really tight?

- Read the words of Jesus, the Shema, and the proverb, sharing how each of those verses helped you think about money.

- Ask each other about questions and exercises you did in the "on your own" section on the previous pages. Remember, this is a conversation with your husband. Get to know him. Listen. Enjoy it!

- Compare your budgets. Did you both do simple or detailed budgets? Talk through the basic realities, obligations, and priorities of how you handle money. Fill in the Our Money Snapshot to get a general picture of your finances. Be sure the numbers "add up" to a realistic lifestyle.

- Go to *Love That Lasts* in your library at *bethkeworkshops.com* and watch this week's video: Money with Matt and Jayne Shatto. They've made money and stewarded it very well, and specifically offer creative ways to walk through the topic of money. After the video, ask each other what was most interesting, most challenging, and a big "takeaway" from the video. Use the video sidebar to take notes and to help your conversation.

The goal here is not to provide a strategy for handling your money, other than to be wise, communicate with one another, and be intentional to pursue your purpose in loving God and others. You may have separate bank accounts; you may share. You may put cash in envelopes; you may use apps to track your spending. There are all kinds of ways to honor God and handle your money with integrity.

So instead of a strategy, the point here is to get a snapshot.

HUSBAND'S INCOME	WIFE'S INCOME
TITHE / GIVING	SAVINGS
HOUSING	SPENDING
TRANSPORTATION	OTHER

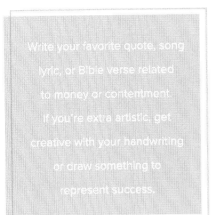

Write your favorite quote, song
lyric, or Bible verse related
to money or contentment.
If you're extra artistic, get
creative with your handwriting
or draw something to
represent success.

Finances with

Matt & Jayne Shatto

This section is a place to take notes if you also purchased the 12 corresponding video sessions from our 12 mentors. What did they say that resonated with you? What was your favorite part? What was most challenging?

_____

_____

_____

_____

_____

_____

_____

_____

_____

_____

_____

_____

_____

_____

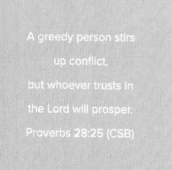

A greedy person stirs
up conflict,
but whoever trusts in
the Lord will prosper.
Proverbs 28:25 (CSB)

If you don't have this video
you can purchase it at

lovethatlasts.co/videoseries

Boundaries

10

A few months ago, Jeff came up the stairs with his mind blown from reading Scott Peck's book *The Road Less Traveled*. He plopped down on the couch and started explaining how restrictions are a really good thing because they, in fact, give us life. If we didn't have restraint and did whatever felt the best or most natural, we'd all poop ourselves! Jeff died laughing on the couch and then went on for twenty minutes on a rant about how true that is. Often times we grumble and complain about restrictions and in our culture today, restrictions are like a bad word. We should be able to do whatever we want. Be free. Live your life. A lot of times, however, our sense of autonomy slowly destroys us.

Our mentors have five kids and live in a duplex. When their two oldest were 13 and 14, they told them they both were going to live on the other side of the duplex for a month. They were expected to pay their own rent, shop for their own groceries, cook their own meals, clean, do their own laundry, and keep up on their homework. They needed to pay their electrical and water bill as well. They were given an allowance and, of course, the bills were very small. The first few days they were there, the 13-year-old boy decided to live it up! He used all their money to buy junk food at the grocery store, stayed up all night playing video games, and left the house a mess. The older daughter was so mad. She had to clean up after him and was baffled that he had spent most of their money on gross food. After a few days though, the boy realized how awful he felt. He was sleep deprived, had a huge stomach ache, and was grossed out with how messy the house was. He missed his mom and her home-cooked meals and how clean the house always was. He quickly learned his lesson and started to handle their money better and use his time better as well. He realized all the "rules" that his parents had set up were actually good and life giving.

In every healthy relationship, each person and couple needs to set up good boundaries in order for the relationship to thrive. There are obvious boundaries like not dating other people and not having an affair, but those things don't just happen overnight. They take time and a lot of forethought. So what boundaries can you put in place to not only protect you as a couple, but to give life to your relationship?

One of my prayers is that the Lord would protect Jeff and I from any little foxes that want to get into our marriage. Song of Solomon 2:15 says, "Catch the foxes for us, the little foxes that spoil the vineyards, for our vineyards are in blossom." Song of Solomon is a story of a man and wife and their wild love for each other. In this verse, Solomon is saying how foxes can get into their marriage to destroy them. They're tricky and small and hard to catch sometimes. And, of course, Satan wants nothing else than to destroy your marriage, and he'll use the smallest little thing to cause you both to be against each other.

In order to protect ourselves from the foxes, we must set up boundaries. The biggest thing is to pray and continue to seek the Lord. As you're walking with Him, you'll be in the light and see the light. You'll be full of self-control and wisdom. It's only when we seek Jesus that we will ever be like Him.

Here are a few practical things that Jeff and I have implemented in our marriage to protect our unity, purity, and joy:

1. Keep communicating. This one is big for me. Often if Jeff and I haven't "connected" in the last 12 hours, I start to read into things, feel lonely, or assume things. I get more defensive or sensitive. It's important for me to connect with him at some point in the day to feel known and to know him. So we try to connect at some point. "How are you? How's your heart? What have you been thinking about today? Anything I can pray for or an area I can serve you in?"

2. Set up intentional time. Often life can run ahead of us, and we're just trying to hold on for dear life! It can seem like Jeff and I are running our own course, instead of running together. Kids make it all the more difficult sometimes to really connect too. We try to set up intentional time in our week, where we know we'll have time just us to connect, rest, and be without interruptions. Sometimes that's a date night where we leisurely talk for a couple hours about anything and everything. Other times it's sitting on the couch, cuddling and reading. Whatever we need during that week where we can be together and remember why we chose one another.

3. Be wise. Know your triggers. This goes with purity and temptation. The reality is that no matter how long you've been married or how much you love Jesus, any one of us can easily be tempted to not choose our spouse. To have a wandering eye. To click on that website. To flirt and have that long text message with someone who isn't our spouse or boyfriend. To fantasize about how your life would be different with another person. Whatever it may be, set yourself up for victory. Know what you struggle with, what you may be prone to, and fight against it. And tell your spouse! Let them know the areas that you struggle in so they can pray with you and keep you accountable. Tell a mentor, get counseling if needed. If there's someone who is flirty with you at work, ask to change departments or be creative about putting yourself in awkward situations. If there's someone who makes you lust at the gym and they're there at the same time every day, don't go during that time. I know it sounds extreme, but those things are extreme. Affairs start small—whether it's a physical affair, emotional affair, or an affair of the mind. Run as fast as you can. Don't go there. Guard your mind. Guard your eyes. Your husband is the only one who should capture your heart and thoughts.

4. Know what gives life to you and your spouse, and what drains it.
This one Jeff and I are still learning, and getting better at each year. And this will morph with us as seasons change. This has to do more with your time and energy level. Every couple is different. Some of us are extroverts, and others introverts. We all need different things and go at different paces. A lot of times one person gets burned out because the other isn't respecting boundaries. Talk about this with your spouse, and find a good way to know when to say yes to things, when to say no, or when to take a rain check. Should you have that family over for dinner? When? How long should your house guests stay with you? Do you need to get a house cleaner so you don't have to be so exhausted after? Should you commit to another activity, a small group, take on another part time job, another payment plan? How can you set yourselves up for rest, joy and success? If you're drowning in some way, feeling exhausted, disconnected, then what needs to change?

GUIDEBOOK

Boundaries

10

66 SO WHEN THEY HAD COME TOGETHER, THEY ASKED HIM, "LORD, ARE YOU RESTORING THE KINGDOM TO ISRAEL AT THIS TIME?"

HE SAID TO THEM, "IT IS NOT FOR YOU TO KNOW TIMES OR PERIODS THAT THE FATHER HAS SET BY HIS OWN AUTHORITY. BUT YOU WILL RECEIVE POWER WHEN THE HOLY SPIRIT HAS COME ON YOU, AND YOU WILL BE MY WITNESSES IN JERUSALEM, IN ALL JUDEA AND SAMARIA, AND TO THE END OF THE EARTH. 99

Acts 1:6-8 (CSB)

The disciples were talking to Jesus forty days after He had raised from the dead. Clearly God was doing something unprecedented. All of the promises they had read in Scripture were coming true. While we know that they were still missing the point of what was happening, their question was more than fair. They're trying to understand. They're excited. They're confused. And any faithful Jew was looking forward to God's kingdom, which Jesus spoke a lot about by the way. (The disciples are so ordinary! It should be really encouraging if you ever wonder if you're good enough or capable of God working in and through your life for his awesome purpose!)

Jesus says that the disciples have a great purpose: They will be his witnesses. They will receive the Holy Spirit. But they don't need to know or worry about all the details—not even the end goal. Jesus didn't say their question was a bad one; it just wasn't one they needed to worry about.

Here's where we see the importance of boundaries, even in good things, in living out God's purpose for your life. Jesus gave them a direction and set a boundary. Don't get sidetracked over here with God's timing. Stay focused on your next steps of obedience in faith. Trust God to do his thing. You do yours.

Boundaries aren't always about sin. Sometimes they're about focus.

What good things distract your attention from what's most important?

_____

_____

_____

What drains your energy and sidetracks you from the purpose you identified for your life?

_____

_____

_____

_____

_____

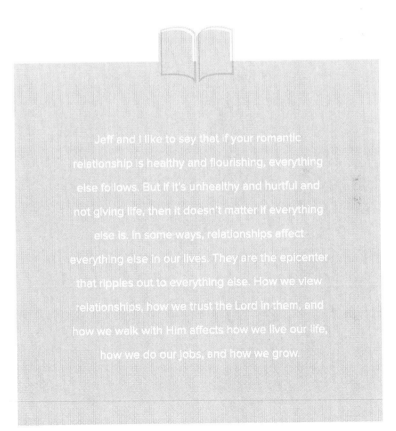

Jeff and I like to say that if your romantic relationship is healthy and flourishing, everything else follows. But if it's unhealthy and hurtful and not giving life, then it doesn't matter if everything else is. In some ways, relationships affect everything else in our lives. They are the epicenter that ripples out to everything else. How we view relationships, how we trust the Lord in them, and how we walk with Him affects how we live our life, how we do our jobs, and how we grow.

ON YOUR OWN

It's possible that you need a change of perspective about boundaries. Many of us do. When you first read the word *boundary* what's your immediate connotation?

positive	negative	neutral

Boundaries are ultimately about protecting what you value. That sounds obvious, but as humans we naturally resist the idea of boundaries. Think back at the story of Adam and Eve again. Everybody knows this part of the story. Adam and Eve are naked and happy in the garden. Life is perfect. God has blessed them and said that they can enjoy everything he has created. There is literally only one boundary set in the universe. The fruit of one tree is off limits. One. And they take it. Bite it. Share it. Together. They believe the lie that joy and freedom are found in a life without boundaries.

We still believe the lie of the serpent that real freedom means doing whatever we want. We want to do what we think is best, regardless of what God may have said. But God clearly sets boundaries for our own good. You wouldn't tell your own kids that they could do whatever they think would make them happy. You need to trust your heavenly Father that he knows what is best for you. Boundaries and order allow things to flourish. He wants you to experience joy.

What boundaries have you currently set in your own life to avoid personal temptation and sin?

_____

_____

_____

What boundaries have you set in your marriage to protect your love?

_____

_____

_____

Being "one" in marriage doesn't mean you have no life or interests of your own. It's healthy and important to have some time to recharge with things you enjoy. Maybe you like to run or workout. Maybe you enjoy basketball or kayaking. Maybe you just need some time at home to read or to work on furniture. It's not selfish to spend a reasonable amount of time doing those things—it's actually good for your marriage.

This is actually a healthy boundary—guarding some time as an outlet and refueling of personal energy. But that same boundary works both ways. Make sure you protect a reasonable amount of time for "your" thing, but don't cross that boundary either, taking too much "me" time.

The key is that the amount of time you spend on "your thing" isn't disproportionate to the amount of time you spend together and that you both agree on what that looks like in your own marriage.

If you're always out with your friends or by yourself, your spouse begins to feel neglected and eventually resentful. Make sure the other person is the priority for your time and energy, but don't stop doing (or discovering) things that you enjoy. Encourage your spouse to take time to do the same.

What do you like to do?

_____

_____

_____

How much time do you spend doing that thing/those things?

_____

_____

_____

What does your husband/wife enjoy?

_____

_____

_____

How much time does he/she spend?

_____

_____

_____

How much time is a reasonable amount for you both to spend on personal interests?

_____

_____

_____

The important thing with boundaries is that they both protect against things that would be bad for you and your marriage, and ensure areas of freedom in things that are good and life-giving. A good gardener—even an all-natural, organic farmer—doesn't allow anything and everything to grow together. A gardener sets boundaries, cultivating growth and health, preventing other things from choking out the good stuff. In other words, boundaries are a good thing. Work with your husband to set healthy boundaries that encourage you to flourish as individuals, as a couple, and as a family.

Yep. Time to turn off or put down your phones. Give each other all of your attention.

- Sit together on the couch or at the table. Start by praying for clarity and transparency for ways to serve one another by protecting each other's hearts and time. Thank God for the gift of someone who loves you so well.
- Read the words of Jesus and the proverb, sharing how each of those verses helped you think about money.
- Ask each other about questions and exercises you did in the "on your own" section on the previous pages. Remember, this is a conversation with your husband. Get to know him. Be honest. Listen carefully. Enjoy it!
- Share with one another what you thought about the suggestions for setting healthy boundaries. What would these look like in your own marriage?
  - Keep communicating.
  - Refuse to speak poorly about each other.
  - No secrets. Ever.
  - Set up intentional time.
  - Know what gives life to you and your spouse, and what drains it.
  - Be wise. Know your triggers.
- What new boundaries need to be set to intentionally focus your lives on God's purpose for you?
- Go to *Love That Lasts* in your library at *bethkeworkshops.com* and watch this week's video: Boundaries with Dave and Ashley Willis. Then ask each other what was most interesting, most challenging, and a big takeaway from the video. Use the video sidebar to take notes and to help your conversation.

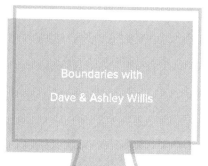

Boundaries with
Dave & Ashley Willis

This section is a place to take notes if you also purchased the 12 corresponding video sessions from our 12 mentors. What did they say that resonated with you? What was your favorite part? What was most challenging?

_____

_____

_____

_____

_____

_____

_____

_____

_____

_____

_____

_____

_____

_____

By wisdom a house is built,
and by understanding it is
established; by knowledge
the rooms are filled with all
precious and pleasant riches.

Proverbs 24:3-4

*If you don't have this video
you can purchase it at*

lovethatlasts.co/videoseries

Dave & Ashley Willis

ON BOUNDARIES

Addiction

11

When God formed humans, He put it in our hearts to worship Him—to adore, praise, exalt, and give all glory to the One and only God who is deserving of all honor. We are created to worship. When sin entered the world, however, we quickly switched to loving everything other than God. God no longer was on the throne of our hearts, being our greatest desire, and the One whom we gave all our affection. Other things replaced Him like money, success, fame, other's approval, porn, body image, control, being comfortable, sex, and the list goes on. We replaced the love of God for the love of idols. We tried to get satisfaction from other things, and gave all our time and energy to those. It broke God's heart; it still breaks God's hearts. And unfortunately, regardless of whether or not we are walking with Jesus, we still have to fight those idols of the heart on the daily because we're made to worship. It's just a matter of what or whom we're worshiping.

These are idols of the heart, and these can easily become addictions in our life. Sure, some are more apparent than others, and some are held as "more sinful" or "really bad" in the church or our culture, but they're all idols of the heart, all things that hurt God's heart and that prevent us from being intimate with Him. We all have idols; it's just a matter of fact. So the question becomes, what are your idols? What do you tend to put on the throne of you heart over God? What do you worship? What do you give your time, energy, thoughts, and money to?

All of these affect our relationships, so we need the right tools to realize what our idols are, confess them, and put them off so we can put on Christ, so we can be our true selves. God has given us people in our lives to help us heal, grow, and change. Sometimes it's only when we're with other people that our idols come out. God has given you your husband or boyfriend to help you become your true self. Not that we put them on a pedestal and they become our savior, but rather they're there to listen, encourage, pray, and sometimes point out areas of our lives that we need to change. And in the same way, you are your husband's person. He is your person. No one knows you better than he does. It's the beauty of marriage. He sees all the good, and all the bad, and in the covenant of marriage, loves you all the same. You need each other and can depend on one another. And in a healthy relationship, you can trust that when either of you confronts the other over something you see in each other's lives that needs to change, you can rest assured that it's out of love.

Now if you're dating, it's a little different because you're not fully each other's "person" yet. You have other people to speak into your life. Mentors. Parents. But you can still have those conversations and need to have those conversations. Be honest with each other. Ask the questions that you don't want to ask. Go there. Be open. Deal in the light. Be humble and kind and open to kind criticism.

Jeff and I had been dating for about two months, when we were driving back from the city one December night. We were holding hands, and my heart was starting to pound in my chest. I knew I needed to tell him my story. My struggle with what felt like my "dark secret." I took a big breath and began telling him that I had struggled with an eating disorder on and off for six years. As the word left my lips, my stomach dropped and I wondered if this would be it. If this would make him love me less or not want to date me anymore. I explained how just four months ago I realized how much my eating disorder hurt the Lord's heart and how it was destroying me. I was on a journey of healing. I still had a long ways to go, but I was repentant, seeking help, and longing to be healed in this area. I was tired of living in slavery, of comparing myself with every girl I saw, of counting calories, not eating with friends because I didn't want them to know. I was over it and longed to be whole. After I got it all out, there was silence. Then Jeff squeezed my hand, and said, "Lyss, thank you so much for telling me that. For entrusting that with me. You're so beautiful, and I'm so excited for you to be fully healed in this area. What can I do to help or what can I be praying for?" It was the sweetest moment for me. To know that I could tell him my ugly stuff, and know that he was in it. He wasn't going anywhere.

During our time dating, we had a few other conversations where Jeff told me of his past and the things he regrets doing. He admitted his porn addiction that lasted up until college, but one that didn't tempt him anymore. It'd been years since he'd looked at porn. We only had a few of those conversations, and during each one, Jeff was honest, and let me ask any question that I needed to. Those conversations are never fun, but they're good and important and, honestly, I think the sooner you have them, the better. If porn is something that he still struggles with, talk with a mentor about what your next step should be. Yes, there is boundless grace, but that doesn't mean that you need to keep dating. He needs to have healing in this area before he is serious about entering into a dating relationship. If you're married and he struggles in this area, pray for him and find help. It's an affair of the mind, and one that can destroy your marriage, but there is hope that he can be healed!

Other addictions could be a love of shopping and spending too much money or being addicted to work, alcohol, busyness, and food. Those are just a few, but pray through what the next steps should be. What is the heart behind those addictions? What are you trying to attain through those? To escape the pain, not deal with the hurt, to be in control, not trusting the Lord? Don't be afraid to ask yourself those questions, and to ask those questions to your significant others. Healing is on the other side, and it is so worth it. God longs to free you, and him.

Maybe there's nothing super apparent right now; some addictions come and go through different seasons. Some are small, and others super obvious. Ask the Lord to search your heart and show you anything that is in your heart that isn't pleasing to Him.

"Let the words of my mouth and the meditation of my heart be acceptable in Your sight O Lord, my Rock and my Redeemer." Psalm 19:14

You are good enough because God sees you through the eyes of Jesus. He covers you. You are worthy because Jesus died for you; He loved you that much and thought you were worth it. Regardless of what type of home you grew up in, what your story is growing up, you have to face these questions and you can face them head on if you have Jesus. Let His word be the final word. You are loved. You are worth it. You are enough. He is so proud of you. He delights in you. You are His.

11

"BUT SEEK FIRST THE KINGDOM OF GOD AND HIS RIGHTEOUSNESS, AND ALL THESE THINGS WILL BE PROVIDED FOR YOU."

Matthew 6:33 (CSB)

In Jesus' greatest sermon, what we call the Sermon on the Mount, He uncovers a wide spectrum of heart issues. He goes idol hunting, shedding light on some of the dark corners of our hearts and minds. Ultimately, stress, worry, addiction, and sin have their roots in worship.

The things we keep going back to, the things that have power in our lives, things that often feel uncontrollable, are things we worship. They're idols. Something inside of us believes the lie that satisfaction, relief, happiness, purpose, acceptance, etc. will be found in this thing other than our Creator. This is the original lie of the serpent in the Garden of Eden. There's a sinful bent in our hearts that doesn't believe that God is good enough. He's holding back on us. We just can't stand the thought of not biting that forbidden fruit. It looks so good.

In Matthew 5-6, Jesus pounds idol after idol:
- Logic and common sense (5:1-12).
- Blending in (5:13-16).
- Self-righteousness (5:17-20).
- Hate and unforgiveness (5:21-26).
- Lust (5:27-30).
- Selfishness, convenience, personal rights (5:31-48)
- Charitable recognition (6:1-4).
- Religious recognition (6:5-18).
- Money, success, and possessions (6:19-24).
- Food, drink, clothing, physical appearance (6:25-34).

Idol after idol after idol, Jesus says that he has something infinitely greater for us. These things that seem so appealing easily seduce our hearts. But Jesus offers us more: He offers true and lasting satisfaction.

Throughout these chapters, Jesus says, "your heavenly Father who sees in secret." God knows. He knows what you think, feel, do, and why you think feel, and do it. He knows your heart.

The fact that Jesus knows all of my secrets

positive	negative

The fact that Jesus loves me even though he knows my secret idols makes me feel...

In the list above, put a check next to the idols you tend to worship.

The verse quoted at the beginning of this section is Jesus' response to our desire for food, drink, and clothing. Jesus says that to put any of these things at the center of our hearts and minds, obsessing over them, worrying about them, seeking them, is a godless thing to do. He promises over and over that God is a perfectly good and generous Father who knows what we need. (Part of knowing our secrets is not only knowing our motives but also our needs.) Jesus promises that if we'll focus our hearts on the goodness of God, seeking his righteousness, first and foremost in our lives, then our heavenly Father will take care of all the things we need and that will give us joy.

He doesn't say food, drink, clothing, wealth, sex, charity, etc are bad. He says that when our focus is on finding meaning and security in those things instead of in him, everything gets bent out of whack. When we can't stop obsessing over them, they'll ruin us. When they become our masters, we'll become enslaved to them. This isn't to be taken lightly or dismissed as a nobody-is-perfect kind of thing. Sin and idolatry are a big, big deal. Look at what Jesus said in the same chapter:

> *If your right eye causes you to sin, gouge it out and throw it away. For it is better that you lose one of the parts of your body than for your whole body to be thrown into hell. And if your right hand causes you to sin, cut it off and throw it away. For it is better that you lose one of the parts of your body than for your whole body to go into hell.*
> *Matthew 5:29-30 (CSB)*

That's intense, but sin is no joke. It's a lie to believe that "as long as I'm not hurting anybody else, then it's not a big deal," or "as long as I only look or think but don't act, it's OK." No. Jesus said to do whatever you have to do to break free from sinful strongholds in your life.

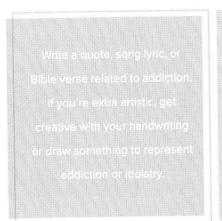

Write a quote, song lyric, or
Bible verse related to addiction.
If you're extra artistic, get
creative with your handwriting
or draw something to represent
addiction or idolatry.

There are seasons where things are going well—you're passionate about God and aware of His activity; relationships are strong; work is satisfying; and free time is enjoyable. When the blessings of God are evident, revel in the freedom and joy of Christ. Each minute is dripping with grace. Soak it up so that you are saturated with peace and spreading His love everywhere you go.

But other days, months, or even years, feel like those same minutes are a suffocating weight under which you are desperately trying to catch a breath that will fill your lungs long enough to sustain you until rescue arrives. It may be easy to believe in your mind that God is good and sovereign, but that doesn't mean you won't find yourself in painful and unfair situations, exhausted, confused, hurting, and at the end of your rope. So what then?

A good way to identify idols and addictions is to look at your patterns of thought or behavior that pop up when you're stressed or drained. Essentially these habitual behaviors have become "functional saviors" that you have an idolatrous love for. You want these idols to validate you, help you, save you. In other words, you look to them for *salvation*.

What do you turn to or "need" when you're under stress?

_____

_____

_____

Underline things that have been past struggles.

Circle current temptations.

Food	Games
Drink	Technology
Drugs	Shopping
Sex	Exercise
Pornography	Work
People	Validation
Social Media	Other:
TV / Movies	

When your marriage isn't in a good spot, what is usually the common theme?

_____

_____

What triggers typically set off addictive patterns or temptations?

_____

_____

_____

What areas of your life do you still need to bring under God's reign and rule?

_____

_____

_____

What boundaries do you need to set—and ask for your husband's help in protecting—to stay focused on God's goodness, His righteousness, His kingdom instead of idolatrous desires and functional saviors?

_____

_____

_____

JOIN TOGETHER

Turn off or put down your phones. (If you haven't noticed, there are surprisingly powerful and addictive behaviors that develop from our phones. How often do you look at them? How hard has it been each week to set them down without looking at them? Do you notice a difference in yourself when you spend more or less time on your phone? Just something to consider.)

Give each other all of your attention. This week is a heavy one, but it's so important.

Some form of addictive behavior has wrecked countless lives and marriages. It's not always something like substance abuse; sometimes it's something like working or neglecting your family because you're always on your phone. But the mentor couple in this week's video will share the difficult road of struggling, confessing, and recovering from an addiction to pornography while in full time ministry. Nobody is bullet proof. Everyone has a target on her back from the enemy, and there's nothing more dangerous than pretending like it isn't there.

- Sit together on the couch or at the table. If you have Jenga, play it for a few minutes for at least one round. If you can't play it, picture the game in your mind and ask each other to explain how the game is played. This is a simple illustration that may be a little cheesy but a fun way to start a tougher topic.
    - The point of the illustration is that each of you has something that may be fine in moderation but could eventually become a problem—even one that could destroy your life and your marriage.
    - Sometimes one slip is all it take to cause a major problem.

- The game has a mixture of fear and adrenaline as you feel compelled to keep doing something. It feels like you're getting away with something every time you don't get busted. This is a great picture of addiction and sinful patterns.

- No matter how good you think you are at handling it—whatever it may be—eventually things will come crashing down. It may be an emotional crash. It could be spiritual. Physical. Relational. Financial. Professional. Legal. But there will always be a crash if we keep playing with destructive patterns.

- We need to encourage one another to stop when we see a pattern that is destructive. Life isn't a game. Cleaning up isn't easy. But if messes have been made in the past, commit to help one another build and guard a new foundation for starting fresh. (This takes trust, communication, and boundaries to a new level of intimacy.)

- Pray together, thanking God for his unconditional love and grace. Ask for Him to fill your hearts with love for Him and for each other in this time of serving one another through compassion and honesty.

- Read the words of Jesus and the proverb, sharing how each of those verses helped you think about addictions.

- Ask each other about questions and exercises you did in the "on your own" section on the previous pages. Remember, this is a conversation with your husband. Get to know him. When he speaks, don't try to "fix." Listen. When you're sharing, be honest and vulnerable. He loves you. You can trust him.

- This is important. Specifically, ask about temptations, patterns, triggers, and common themes when things are bad.

- Help each other identify healthy boundaries to guard one another's hearts and minds so that you can seek the goodness and freedom of life under the authority of a loving Father and King.

- Go to *Love That Lasts* in your library at *bethkeworkshops.com* and watch this week's video: Addiction with Bernie and Christina Anderson. Then ask each other what was most interesting, most challenging, and a big takeaway from the video. Use the video sidebar to take notes and to help your conversation.

- Be sure to make note of the resources linked under the video for more insights on specific issues. These are invaluable resources for you and for people you know.

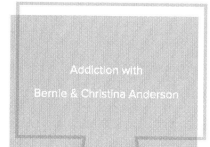

Addiction with

Bernie & Christina Anderson

This section is a place to take notes if you also purchased the 12 corresponding video sessions from our 12 mentors. What did they say that resonated with you? What was your favorite part? What was most challenging?

_____

_____

_____

_____

_____

_____

_____

_____

_____

_____

_____

_____

_____

Can a man embrace fire and his
clothes not be burned?
Can a man walk on burning coals
without scorching his feet?
Proverbs 6:27-28 (CSB)

If you don't have this video

you can purchase it at

lovethatlasts.co/videoseries

Rhythms

12

Jeff has introduced me to rhythms in our marriage, and I am slowly learning to not only love them, but I also greatly depend on them. I've always been a person who loves routine. I love spontaneity too, but in the day to day, I need routine. I thrive with routine and without it, I can easily crumble. I could tell you all about our routine, of when my kids wake up, when nap time is, when we eat. But there are three things that are foundational to my routine each day that give me life. Routine is just how you go about your day, your schedule. But rhythms are built on things that build you up, refresh you, and are important to you.

On an ideal day (I'm a mom with littles, so things don't always go as planned. Well, actually I'm human so things definitely don't always go as planned!), I like to wake up an hour before the kids and sit with my coffee and read and pray and journal. I need this built into my day one way or another. (Sometimes it looks like me quickly reading a psalm on my iphone while my oldest plays quietly with Legos for 5 minutes, and my youngest has found something to chew on that's surprisingly keeping him preoccupied for a few minutes.) I love going for a walk to clear my head and listen to a sermon a few times a week. And I need to go to bed at a decent time, and relatively the same time, every night so I can be my best for the kids the next day. Those three things, I'm learning, are really important for my week.

I also like to be able to read throughout the week to refresh and fill up. I love taking naps when my kids do, and I love having special time with my husband when the kids go to bed. I know we all can look at our lives and find things that we need to do each day, or each week that give us life and help to ground us.

Rhythm, is like a tempo that you build into your marriage and family, that gives you life and refreshment. It's a lot like routine, but more big picture. If you look back at the Old Testament, you can see tons of rhythms that God built into the Jewish lifestyle that was for their flourishing. Sabbath, where one day a week they ceased from all work and rested and worshiped and feasted and refueled. Holidays, where they celebrated, gathered, looked back and remembered. Every seventh year, they let their land go, giving it a rest from harvesting and cultivating. And in Leviticus 25, God tells the people of Israel that every 50 years, they are to have a year of Jubilee where all the slaves and prisoners are set free and debts are forgiven.

I think in our Western, American culture, we've let rhythms fall aside in exchange for busyness and work and ultimately, not trusting the Lord. We often can think we always have to be doing. Always have to be producing. Or the one day we have off, we need to catch up on errands. I believed this and lived it out for years. But God is calling us into something so much greater. He is our good Shepherd and loves to give us rest and rejuvenation. I'm learning, however, that those don't just come about. We have to plan for them, and sometimes it feels like we have to move mountains for them to happen, but it's always worth it!

The things that important to my routine—working out, spending time in God's word, and going to bed at a decent time—don't just happen, especially as a mom. I have to plan for them and sometimes sacrifice for them. I don't always feel like working out, but I know that when I'm done, I feel refreshed and am a better mom and wife because of it. I also don't always wake up yearning to read my Bible, but I know that I need to hear from Jesus when it's just me and him in the quietness of my home so I get up early. And I have to really work hard to go to bed a decent time, which means getting off of my phone 30 minutes before bed, stopping cleaning my house or reorganizing or going for a late errand run, to snuggle into bed and read before my eyelids give way because I know I need the sleep and if my baby wakes up teething in the middle of the night, I'll be ready.

Those are just for me. So I can be the best mom and wife and woman that I can be. Jeff and I have talked a lot about rhythms in our marriage and family, and it's taken years for us to figure out what we need and how to implement them. We're still trying to figure it out, and I'm sure it'll change in some way with whatever season we're in .

So for our family, Sabbath once a week is a rhythm that is necessary and good. This means we turn off our phones at dinner time. Then we make a big celebratory meal and sing a song with the kids. Then Jeff says a blessing over each kid and looks them in the eye while he tells them something he saw and celebrated in them this week, or simply things he loves about them. We then light a candle that we keep burning all the way until dinner the next night. The next morning we do a special breakfast, and then usually go to the beach or outside for some refreshing activity. Sabbath for us is about ceasing and celebrating. So that's what we do.

We also have come to cherish date nights. With two littles in the house, it can be hard sometimes to have intentional time together where it's just us, and we're fully present. Because often we just want to fall on the couch by 8pm and not talk for an hour and then go to bed! We're learning to put it on the calendar as well, to get a babysitter in advance, even if it's just for an hour. We need it. And we're trying to spend special time with each of our kids each week too. We like dating them as well. Getting to know their hearts. Doing what they love doing.

Within rhythms, we're also learning to give ourselves a whole lot of grace. Because things don't always go as planned. Some seasons are a lot busier than others, so we have to let some things go, or plan ahead even better. Some days my babies' are teething or are sick. There are tantrums or illness or people that may need us. A meal needs to be dropped off, we need to take a trip to the doctors. So grace on all of us, but it's worth it. Our weekly day off draws us closer together as a family. We let go of our daily tasks. We serve each other. We do what refreshes us individually and as a family. And it doesn't just come naturally (yet!). We put it on the calendar and plan and prepare for it. Just like a holiday, really. And now I get why God built that in, why He commanded it. Because it's so good. And needed. Every week.

GUIDEBOOK

Rhythms

12

"BUT THE NEWS ABOUT [JESUS] SPREAD EVEN MORE, AND LARGE CROWDS WOULD COME TOGETHER TO HEAR HIM AND TO BE HEALED OF THEIR SICKNESSES. YET HE OFTEN WITHDREW TO DESERTED PLACES AND PRAYED."

Luke 5:15-16 (CSB)

Not only was Jesus a busy and important man, He was God. Yet, Jesus often withdrew to deserted places and prayed. The whole idea that we're too busy to pray or to spend time quietly resting in the presence of God is absurd. No matter what is on your checklist for the day, week, month, or year, it isn't miraculously healing and teaching to mobs of people who follow you around.

The fact that Jesus was God doesn't make the constant demand on His time and energy any less human. He grew tired. But notice the fact that Jesus was God didn't mean He felt exempt from the need to have this pattern of public and private time. Jesus had a steady rhythm in his life. Steady doesn't necessarily mean structured to the point of never changing his daily routine. But his rhythm was one of loving God and loving the people around him. Love God. Love people. Love God by loving people. Love people by loving God.

Sometimes the most loving thing we can do for people is to spend time alone with God for a bit before returning to them. Jesus didn't stay in the deserted places, but he often withdrew from the public into privacy.

To stress the importance of having healthy spiritual rhythms, consider the first part of the verses above. Jesus was healing people and teaching huge crowds the truth about God. It would've been the world's greatest conference and Bible study! What could be more important than the Son of God healing people and preaching the truth of the kingdom? Sometimes, according to Jesus, being alone in personal prayer was more important than being with the crowds.

The only Son of God. In His short life on earth and a mere three-year ministry. With the power to heal, cast out demons, and even raise the dead. Sometimes the best use of Jesus' time was to be alone. Praying. This was a rhythm in his life and ministry.

Write your favorite quote, song lyric, or Bible verse related to rhythm, longevity, or beauty. If you're extra artistic, get creative with your handwriting or draw something to represent rest, joy, or life.

ON YOUR OWN

Once again we can look all the way back to the first pages of Scripture to see this beautiful truth of the God-given gift of rhythms. In fact we look back to the very first hours, so to speak.

In creation we see God establish and bless two rhythms. First we read over and over in Genesis 1, *There was an evening, and there was a morning: one day.* Two. Three. Four. Five. Six. Day after day there is this rhythm and order to all of creation. Dark. Light. Quiet. Activity. Good. Good. Good. Good. Good. Good.

And then this song builds to its crescendo.

> *So the heavens and the earth and everything in them were completed. On the seventh day God had completed his work that he had done, and he rested on the seventh day from all his work that he had done. God blessed the seventh day and declared it holy, for on it he rested from all his work of creation.*
> *Genesis 2:1-3 (CSB)*

The most significant part of a rhythm, what defines it, what makes it beautiful, setting it apart from all other noise is the intentional rest. Without the rest, it's just sound. It's noise. It's chaos. But rest breaks up the frenzy of activity into something meaningful. Suddenly it makes sense. It takes a shape and moves our hearts. Noise becomes music.

God created you to flourish as a man created in His image. It's vital to break up the noise in your life with intentional rest. Establish rhythms—personally and in your marriage. If you have kids, establish family rhythms too.

Describe your ideal day (ideal but real-life scenario).

_____

_____

_____

Now describe your typical day.

_____

_____

_____

What natural patterns do you have in your day?

_____

_____

_____

What moments of rest and focus can you add to your routine to bring order and meaning to your day?

_____

_____

_____

Do you regularly practice the following things and if so, when?

pray ◇◇◇◇◇◇◇◇◇◇◇◇◇◇◇◇◇◇◇◇◇◇◇◇ when _____

read the Bible ◇◇◇◇◇◇◇◇◇◇◇◇◇◇◇◇ when _____

worship in a church ◇◇◇◇◇◇◇◇◇◇◇◇ when _____

share life in a small group ◇◇◇◇◇◇◇ when _____

practice generosity ◇◇◇◇◇◇◇◇◇◇◇◇◇ when _____

eat together ◇◇◇◇◇◇◇◇◇◇◇◇◇◇◇◇◇◇ when _____

mentor / disciple ◇◇◇◇◇◇◇◇◇◇◇◇◇◇ when _____

other: _____ when _____

other: _____ when _____

other: _____ when _____

The seventh day of the week, the holy day God blessed is called the *Sabbath.* In the original Hebrew language, the word means to cease. The point here is not about a legalistic practice of not doing certain things on a certain day. The heart of Sabbath is rest and worship. It's focusing our hearts on God. He is the one who created everything. We can trust him enough to be rest in his goodness. Sabbath isn't lazy or legalistic, it's an organic liturgy. It's a natural ordering of our worship through rhythms in life.

Over the past 12 weeks, you've been developing rhythms. You've read on your own, thought through things on your own, and spent time with each other (hopefully no phones or distractions). You've had fun and probably had some difficult spots too. That's good. Most important, we hope that these rhythms have led you to meaningful conversations and deeper intimacy, loving God and loving one another with all of your hearts, minds, souls, and strength.

- Sit together on the couch or at the table. Start by talking about your favorite rhythms as a couple or family. Share why you enjoy those routines.
- Read the words of Jesus and the proverb, sharing how each of those verses helped you think about rhythms.
- Ask each other about the lists, activities, and intentional times of rest you identified in the "on your own" section on the previous pages. Pay attention to your husband's natural rhythms and those that he desires.
- Complete the Our Rhythms section below, identifying ways that you can be intentional with your time as individuals, as a couple, and as a family. (You may want to do this now while it's fresh, or after the video when you have some more input from your video mentors.)
- Go to *Love That Lasts* in your library at *bethkeworkshops.com* and watch this week's video: Rhythms with John Mark and Tammy Comer. Then, ask each other what was most interesting, most challenging, and a big takeaway from the video. Use the video sidebar to take notes and to help your conversation.
- Finish your time together by identifying a favorite or most helpful takeaway from each of the past 12 sessions. As you do, consider how

what you've experienced can become a natural part of your rhythm in love and marriage.

- If you're not yet in community with other Christians, don't rob yourself of this incredible joy. Your church community truly is the next most important relationship in your life next to your marriage. Remember, God created us for relationships. You need people around you to share the joys and the struggles of faith—people who will encourage you in your rhythms as the days, weeks, months, and years roll along. God's people are His masterpiece. His church is His bride. He made you for love. Everybody wants a love that lasts.

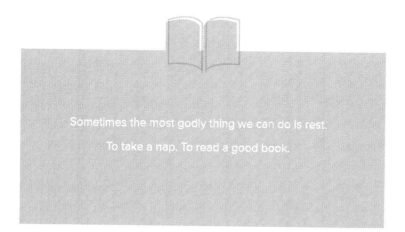

Sometimes the most godly thing we can do is rest.
To take a nap. To read a good book.

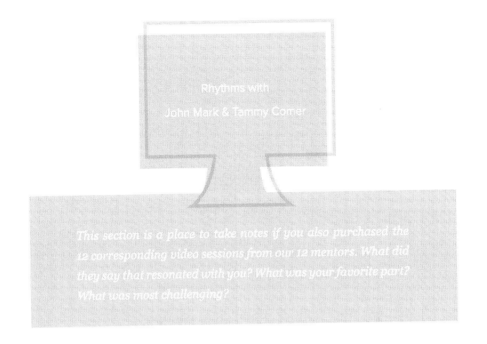

Rhythms with

John Mark & Tammy Comer

This section is a place to take notes if you also purchased the 12 corresponding video sessions from our 12 mentors. What did they say that resonated with you? What was your favorite part? What was most challenging?

Above all else, guard
your heart,
for everything you do
flows from it.
Proverbs 4:23 (NIV)

OUR RHYTHMS

Write down things that are needed for a healthy rhythm as individuals, a couple, and as a family. Then, identify times within your daily or weekly schedule that you can intentionally prioritize the things that everyone needs in their healthy rhythms. (For example, if you need to spend 20 minutes reading your Bible and praying by yourself, and the best time to be alone is at 6am, then mark those down.) Identify as many or as few as you need to right now. This is just another tool to help you start thinking intentionally about establishing healthy rhythms in your life!

	NEEDS	TIME
HUSBAND		
WIFE		
COUPLE		
FAMILY		

OUR TAKEAWAYS

1. theology of marriage

2. trust

3. communication

4. conflict

5. faith

6. purpose

7. sex

8. parenting

9. finances

10. boundaries

11. addiction

12. rhythms

Let us know what you think! We'd love to hear from you!

#LoveThatLasts

A Final Word to Our Friends

You made it! Congrats! We know it wasn't easy. First, we wanted to extend a genuine and heartfelt thank you for taking this journey with us.

Second, we'd love to hear your feedback. You can say hi at our social links below, or if you use the hashtag #LoveThatLasts, we tend to click on that every so often and hop in the conversation with you.

We pray that you were encouraged as you went through them. I know they were deeply encouraging for us to write and work through. There's nothing like the power of grace and the love of Jesus to revitalize or strengthen any relationship out there. And don't forget that the secret of a healthy marriage, grace, is less like a flu shot and more like oxygen. It's something we need every second of every day to succeed, not just something we find once and then never come back for.

So rest in God's grace and love for you and your spouse (or significant other). He sees you. He knows you. He is with you.

Jeff & Alyssa

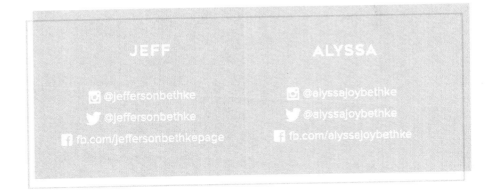

JEFF

@jeffersonbethke
@jeffersonbethke
fb.com/jeffersonbethkepage

ALYSSA

@alyssajoybethke
@alyssajoybethke
fb.com/alyssajoybethke

#LoveThatLasts

One of the secrets to a healthy relationship is it needs to be fed for it to grow. No relationship becomes healthy, vibrant or joyful from complacency. In fact, the minute proactivity leaves the relationship is the minute it can begin to breakdown. In 31 Creative Ways To Love And Encourage Him and Her Jefferson and Alyssa Bethke lay out simple ways to bring the beauty, joy and vibrancy back to a relationship. Each day brings a new adventure that can range from being serious to whimsical to humerous. Take this one month journey with your spouse or significant other and come out the other side with a stronger and more healthy relationship than before.

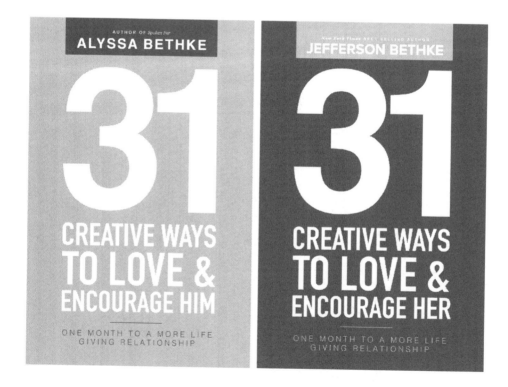

GET $10 OFF

(normally 32.99 for the bundle)

at shop.jeffandalyssa.com

by using code

"LOVETHATLASTS"

at checkout.

START A MARRIAGE SMALL GROUP

You can do the love that lasts journey in a group setting. Average is $60 per couple. Normal price is $144.

Start your group at

shop.jeffandalyssa.com

JEFF & ALYSSA BETHKE

10% off entire store with code '10percent' at shop.jeffandalyssa.com

CEO
CHEF
LIFEGUARD
CHAUFFEUR
PSYCHOLOGIST
ART DIRECTOR
AKA MOM

WHAT
CAN I SAY
EXCEPT
YOU'RE
WELCOME

I'M SO IN
LOVE
WITH MY
HUSBAND

I'D RATHER BE
DRINKING
COFFEE
& READING
A BOOK

50442876R10167

Made in the USA
San Bernardino, CA
23 June 2017